Tune In

Fauntee's Inspirational Quotes for Success

FAUSTINA ANYANWU

Copyright 2018 © by Faustina Anyanwu.
Published by Faunteewrites Limited.

Royal Arsenal Gatehouse, London, SE18 6AR. United Kingdom.

Faustina Anyanwu asserts her right to be identified as the author of this work in accordance with the copyright, designs and patent Act 1988. All rights reserved. No part of this publication may be reproduced, stored in a retrieval system, or transmitted, in any form or by means, electronic, mechanical, photocopying, recording or otherwise, without the prior written permission of the copyright owner.
A CIP catalogue record for this book is available from the British Library.

ISBN: 9780993041730
© A Faunteewrites Limited Imprint. 2018.

CONTENTS

Dedication...7
Acknowledgement......................................9
Introduction...11

Section One – Background story...............13
Difficulty Shaped my Life............................17
Without a Dad...18
Going it alone..20
Dad came back into my life.........................22
The Struggle Continues...............................23
Finding my Path..26
Out of My path..29
My Why...32
My ideals...35
Making the right choices.............................36

Section Two – Poetry...............................39
Introduction..41
Dad Never was there...................................43
We are Humans...45
All in my heart..49
My little Girl...51
When I see your smile.................................52
How About Now..53

I love you more	56
The boy with the hood	59
My only Star	61
They all say No	62
One At A Time	64
The End is Nigh	66
Hello New Year	68
The Great Britain	70
The Morning Breeze	72
My Mother	75
I don't want to talk	76
You have a choice	78
It's just a dream	81
For all that you gave me	83
The Sojourner's Dialogue	84
Summer	89
Will	90
They will Never See	91
The Refugee	92
The Beauty of Nature	94
God	95
Pundiyaya	97
It's Winter Again	99
A Soldier's Day to Love	101
Lord you are Good	103

TUNE IN

Section Three – Quotes for Success. **105**

Section Four – Thoughts on Success. **129**
Finding Success. 131
Building the skills. 136
The Power of Mentorship 137

Section Five – Entrepreneurship **143**
No Need to Fear 145
Three Advice for Startups 146
Skills for a successful Millennial Entrepreneur 147
Becoming a Successful Entrepreneur 147
Building a Successful Customer Base 147
Managing Expectations, Challenges and Reality for successful Relationships. 148

Section Six – 14 Steps to Success **153**
Step 1 – Understanding yourself. 157
Step 2 – Self Love and Acceptance. 159
Step 3 – Define your Purpose. 161
Step 4 – Start from where you are 163
Step 5 – Give your best 165
Step 6 – Surround yourself with like minds 169
Step 7 – Never Make any mistake twice. 171
Step 8 – Listen to every advice but take only yours. 173
Step 9 – Always Have a Plan B. 175

Step 10 – Be Who You Are At All Times. 177
Step 11 – Do your Best and leave the rest. 179
Step 12 – Be Willing to Fail 181
Step 13 – Beware of Get rich quick schemes 183
Step 14 – Be Teachable – Learn from your juniors. 185

Section Seven – Thought on Capitalism. 187

DEDICATION

I dedicate this book to my beloved husband for his patience, dedication, love and encouragement all our 12 years together. You are the only human being who understands me, my needs and truly knows who I am. Your support, encouragement and resilience have been my bedrock. Thank you so much.
I will always love you, my GS.

GS. xx.

ACKNOWLEDGEMENT

I wish to sincerely and deeply thank everyone who has been part of shaping my life.

To the Almighty God, who has been my guidance at every turn. He hasn't ever left me, even at my darkest hours. For turning every wrong in my life to my stepping stone and making me see in all my situations His hand in my life.

My indebted gratitude goes to my Mum, Mrs Cordelia Uche (Nee Nwagwu). You remain the greatest influencer in my life and you have always been my role model. Your willingness to put your feet down, forgo your own life for me to thrive, your every tears and fear. Today, through this book, God has rewarded you. I will forever remain grateful and loyal to your motherly love and trust.

To my siblings: this is our story. You all can attest to each and every word in this book. I'm exceptionally proud of you all. My elder brother, Reginald Uche; my immediate younger sister, Mrs Vivian Amanze; my second little sister, Mrs Chinwe Anyanwu and our little baby, Uche Emma Nonso. No situation has ever broken our bond and loyalty for each other. We all have worked incredibly hard to be each other's support network. All our individual achievements have come together to be our collective stepping stone of an undefeatable strength. I love you all with all my heart.

To all my friends, my business associates, and everyone who has helped me in any way to keep thriving: I will forever remain grateful. This is especially extended to Ms. Gayle Ngozi Igwebike,

Thee Late Dr. Nkem Ezeilo, Mrs. Caroline Popoola, Prince Eze Ihenacho, Dr. Brighton Chireka, Professor Rotimi Jaiyesimi, Chief Ayo Oyebade, and Mr. Geoffrey Odur. I'm most grateful to Vee Roberts who gave me the nudge to put my thoughts into a book. This book is your baby too. Thank you.

I appreciate also those who have made things difficult for me sometimes. You helped me learn how to do things better and achieve the best results. I love you all.

Last but not the least, my greatest love and gratitude extends to my family: my husband, Emeka Anyanwu, Dii, you know everything. We have been on this long, beautiful journey together in every way. To my daughters, Chelsea, Danielle and Jidechi: you all are wonderful children. My conversations with you have been a source of wisdom and eye opening. You all give my life so much meaning and have made me appreciate life even more. I love you so much with all of my heart.

INTRODUCTION

Knowledge is everywhere. Wisdom is rare, just as you're about to discover. Tune in for an overflow of my many original, inspiring and powerful quotes. This is a collection of my original poems and thoughts. It's a window into my life journey as I discover the true meaning of success. It's a deep opening into a life that has been discovered, shared and learnt about to be re-discovered and ultimately a life that is determined to leave traces for others to walk through in their own discovery.

The words in this book will tune you into an uncontrollable drive to success. It is with words that will help you shift in your business, career or personal life. This book will awaken and equip you with affirmations, motivation and handy advices on every aspect of your journey to becoming the person you dream of becoming. I would like you to see this book as a practical guide on how to tune in on success and living. You will be able live life on your own terms through honest self discovery, while being truthful to yourself.

This book is filled with memorable actionable quotes, drawn from deep personal experiences. When life begins to throw all what it has at you, challenges, pressures, frustrations and despair. Tune In gives you a clear lens with which to deal, embracing and profiting from these deep and personal life stretches. The purpose of this book is to awaken you to the truth so that you are Tuned Into the positives: joy, happiness, fulfillment and the drive to succeed. You have been equipped with the most precious thing – life filled with experiences that taught you it can be done.

SECTION ONE – MY BACKGROUND STORY

Note

Most of the things in which you will read here are the circumstances that probably formed the person of whom I am today. I no longer feel vulnerable telling my story. I hope that my opening up to you will draw you into my mind so that we can share a meaningful journey of getting out of the pod. It's essential that we leave the baggage behind so that we can Tune In to a future full of opportunities in which we are to discover and own. My Mum taught me to do that long before I knew what I was doing; it has paid off. I'm here to help you do the same. If I did it then you can too!

Come with me.
@Fauntee xx.

TUNE IN

Difficulty shaped my life

The purpose of this book is to help you tune into your journey, while making the best out of the difficult times in your life. Often times, we get drowned into our problems. We fail to see the opportunities which they bring. I am just like everyone else without my story; we all have a story to tell. What is important in our stories, isn't to tell tales of difficulty so that we are pitied, but rather to inspire the reader. People tell stories to pick themselves up and dust themselves off. It provides a way to learn from your own journey. They can make the necessary changes in which feel they need to be.

The biggest lessons from my childhood are:

- That I can be resourceful.
- Not to depend on anyone.
- That I can change my life and not make the same mistakes my parents made.
- To pay attention to my environment, myself and my situations.
- That I can become extraordinary.
- That my background has nothing to do with who I become.
- Helped me see the beauty in nature and appreciate the presence of God more.
- It helped me discover my hidden talents and how to tap into my being.

- My journey taught me how not to be carried away by frenzy and material things.
- It gave me opportunity to discover and fall in love with books. I discovered rare gems like Nelson Mandela, Oprah Winfrey, Maya Angelou and Jesus Christ.

There are also some weaknesses that I adopted from being exposed to certain experiences. Still, I grew despite these weaknesses. I learnt to turn them into stepping stones. There are so many of them hidden in my poems, in my quotes and in my thoughts. I hope that you can pick them up and use them for your own best.

Without a Dad

I was only four years old when my parents separated in July 1982. You see, life doesn't have regard for your age. Things you never participated in could form your reality. A four-year-old, of whom her father isn't there, causes her life to start onto a different path, despite what my Mum and her parents were able to do for I and my siblings. Being the first daughter, quickly responsibilities rested on my tiny shoulders. My fragile shoulders suddenly became stronger. I had to learn very quickly. My grandmother used to tell us, "Know which look is a wink, gaze or scowl."

The words of my grandmother have ever since lived with me. I have been a careful observer of how life turns. I have also been a deep thinker. At every point in time, I observe people around me, events and situations. I take everything in and chew them over in my mind's eye. You should be doing this, too.

My earliest memory was the day we left my Dad. I can't quite recall what happened earlier or why we were leaving. . Yet, I can still vividly remember that it was dark at night. With hindsight, I believe it was early morning; maybe around 4 or 5am. We had walked through a narrow road to come out onto the major tarred road, what I now know to be the Owerri – Umuahia road. I remember seeing a huge, bright light beam at us. I don't recall anything else between that time and when we got to the home of my Mum's aunty. However, I recall being woken up. We were taken into a Peugeot pick up van that took us to my grandparents. I later would learn that those were my grandpa's vehicles. My Mum was bulging with pregnancy of my second sister who was born that same week as we arrived my maternal home.

My maternal home was a large, popular family. My grandfather's house, his brothers and other relatives lived in the same huge compound. My grandparents were tobacco merchants. His elder brother was a retired headmaster, and his younger brother was signatory to Nigerian currency. Their mother, my great-grandma, was the daughter to the King of the nearby village. She was a Princess. The family was, and still is, one of the most popular families in my state.

Going it Alone

All my life I've worked so hard and I've tasted both sides of life.

I had a wealthy father, an educated mother and wealthy maternal grandparents. Yet, growing up to experience poverty equipped me with so much experience.

I've always taken action to go get almost everything I've achieved in my life.

I remember when we were at my maternal home at the age of five. One early morning, I decided it was time for me to start school. I'd had enough of having to baby-sit my youngest sister. My Mum was at school then for her NCE and my grandparents went to market. They were tobacco merchants.

I hadn't discussed this with anyone so nobody knew what was coming — not even my elder brother, of whom I planned to follow up with my plans. That morning I went to the backyard and picked one of the leftover planks as my slate. I left for school following my brother. I can't remember now how he reacted, but I did get to school somewhat by myself.

During registration, I told them my name as Faustina Uche and that was it. I started school that day.

My Mum usually comes home every Friday; she heard I started school upon getting home. I don't know what her reaction was; all I remembered was that she wanted to be sure I used my Igbo name to register. She asked in a line like, "I hope you're answering Chidinma?" I said, "No, I registered with Faustina." She racked and that was it. I loved my 'strange' name as it was called then. I used to be the only one with the name while I was at school; maybe once or twice there will be one more person called Faustina. I loved my name.

You see, right from childhood, I've always had my own mind. I knew exactly what I wanted from life. I make decisions that won't please everyone. But I made sure at least that it was exactly what I believed was right for me. In the end, though, my decisions have always brought smiles to people's faces. Sometimes, though, they won't want to admit it to my face or in public.

I started babysitting my youngest sister at the age of four; and, I could cook at the age of six. I bathed my sisters and was fully responsible for them when Mum was at school. My grandmother was a legend. She is super strong and industrious. She was wealthy and well-known. She helped so many people, and she trained so many in school. My maternal home used to have over 20 people at all times eating from my grandma's kitchen at every meal.

She knew how to delegate and get results. So it was my direct duty to care for my sisters and to report to her of any issues as soon as she's back from market . This was how we operated during the week. My Mum would come home on the weekends and, for once, I'd become a child again. I loved Friday evenings, Saturday and early Sundays. Our lives will suddenly change by 4pm Sunday. Mum would be going back to school and I'd have to grow up again.

FAUSTINA ANYANWU

Dad Came back in my life

Seven years after my parents separated (1989), I and my Mum and siblings were living at my Mum's posting. She worked there as a teacher. One hot afternoon, my Dad appeared from nowhere. I and my siblings were excited. We were young and didn't have any idea what was going on. We persuade my Mum to reconcile with Dad. After several other visits and pleading from everyone, my Mum reunited with my Dad. I believed and trusted that my Dad was genuinely back for good. But, guess what?

Your guess is as good as mine. I had the first shocker of my life. I had taken exams for special secondary schools. I passed and got admission to attend Mercy Juniorate, a prestigious catholic convent secondary school. I had only gone for the first term and we went for holidays. As my Mum was preparing for us to finally move back to my Dad, she decided I go straight from school to my dad's house. It was the defining moment in my life. I was only 12 years at this time (1990). I didn't know anyone in my village except my Dad. I was hopeful and excited to spend time with him, possibly bond and start a new chapter in our lives.

My Dad abandoned me to my dismay. You would not know his whereabouts for several days and weeks. He would not keep any money for me to eat. I didn't know who to contact or how to reach my Mum. I continued to endure. The final straw for me was this: I was to go back to school. My Mum had told her schoolmate, whose daughter was also in the school, to pick me up on her way from taking her daughter back to school. It was at the end of the term break. However, on that fateful day, my Dad told me to ask them to go. He will drive me back to school. Till today , I'm still waiting for my Dad to take me back to that school.

My school at Mercy Juniorate ended. Of course, the school is highly disciplined. You are automatically rusticated if you don't come back to school on the resumption date (without a good reason). Even if I had any chance of explaining my absence from school and getting back to school, distance and time played into my Dad's hands. It was almost two months before my Mum came back from her school. She found me sitting in the house. She could not believe her eyes. My Mum was angry. She was bitter, she cried, and she screamed. Because I took my common entrance exam at a different local government and I have been in a private school, it became a tug of war to get me back to another school in my local government. My Mum, from that minute, embarked on the fight to get me into one of the highest ranking schools around. She travelled to the state capital almost everyday and she was now heavily pregnant with my youngest brother. A few times when she couldn't go by herself, she delegated to one of my cousins; my Dad's elder sister's son.

The Struggle

She was able to get me into Ogbor Girls (formerly Regina Caeli) after a long battle. Mum finally concluded her transfer to come back to my town. She was finally posted to our neighbouring village. The bad road meant she spent about 45 minutes to one hour each day traveling on public cyclist to the school. One day, while going to school, my Mum fell off the bicycle and her entire body fell flat on her back into a muddy water. She had to rush back. School was cancelled for the day. My sisters began school at a nearby primary school too.

It wasn't long that we were about to settle in our new home; then, the war began again. Every single day we would find my Mum crying. She did her best to hide all that was going on. But there is not much you can hide from such inquisitive children as the situation worsened.

My Mum began to miss school. Most times my mum's hair will look unkempt. We won't have anything to eat. My Mum looked scared and worn out. I remember discussing these worries with my sister Ndidi. We wondered why Mum wasn't taking care of herself again. We didn't go out except for going to school. We stopped going to church. My Mum was nothing like the woman I grew up to know. She was a stranger in how she looked and behaved.

One day I summoned courage to confront her. I remember the discussion going something like: "Mum, you have changed. What is wrong with you?" She tried to hide her face but I saw she was crying. I then called my sister and we continued to press her to know what was wrong. I remember asking her why she no longer fixed her hair, and why we always never had food again. Mind you, at this time Mum was heavily pregnant, about six months. What she could get herself to say was that she was pregnant and that my

Dad had taken all her money. We asked her why. She explained that she had to surrender her salary every month to avoid trouble. We challenged her. We suggested to her for us to go back to where we lived before, which was where she used to teach. I can't remember how that discussion ended. But I can say that it sparked something in her. I believe that day she took a decision for our sake. The next salary, I believe my Mum refused to surrender it and that was when hell broke. The fight and verbal abuse began. I witnessed it all each time. I was bitter and I was angry. I was confused. At this time my brother was already in the seminary (boarding school). He wasn't aware of what was going on. But I saw it all. I experienced all of it.

One fateful night, the fight began again. My dad had pushed my pregnant Mum face down. I could no longer take it. I used a plank which I found there and hit him on the back. As I did, my Dad took a machete and chased me through the night. I ran as fast as my legs could take me. That gave my Mum the opportunity to pick my two sisters and run away. After the incident, we all had enough. It was time for my Mum to save her own life and that of her children. She had to find a house in our neighbouring village where her school was. We began to live there again, while leaving everything we owned. This move meant that I had to walk to and from that village back to my village each day where my school was. This went on for about two to four months. Thankfully, I was never harmed walking to and from the narrow bushy roads to and back from school each day.

FAUSTINA ANYANWU

Finding my Path

I was helpless while growing up in an abusive and confusing home. My Dad hit my Mum, which lead us to runaway from comforts. I was more confused and I blamed myself often, wishing there was ways I could help myself (or my Mum) out of our situation. We often faced bullying while at school. When other children would tease us saying, "Why don't you go back to your father's house?" "You think I don't know your Dad beats your Mum and that's why you are here." Sometimes, other children will not allow you to participate in their plays because 'you don't have a Dad.' I learnt to stand up for myself. I and my siblings became closely knitted together. I was often defensive and scared of people. I doubted everyone's intention towards me. I think it was the combination of these confusing environments that gave me the drive to become more focused and doing everything. I could to prove myself and also help me to understand the feelings of others.

At about the age of 12 to 13, I began to pick interest in poetry and sports. I was writing sporadically and participated in all school sports. I would always be the best. I came first all the time. Writing became my getaway. The little girl who used to talk too much telling stories became withdrawn. I became an emotional wreck. I was hypersensitive, anxious and would cry for anything. I still do. Disappointments began to feel like a stab in the heart. I didn't want to have friends anymore. I avoided having friends because I didn't want them to come to my house and discover my family situation. I didn't talk about my Dad or family. I could be friendly with everyone but never had a close friend. I became timid. The stigma followed me. I always believed everyone knew about my parents. It was the most difficult way to be a teenager. I was so protective of my Mum, my siblings and myself. I was afraid and suspicious of people. The only time I could be myself was with my siblings and family.

My only way of getting to my heart was to write down my thoughts, usually as poems. I learnt to study hard. I made sure I was in the top best student at all times. I was always the teachers favourite.

I used to have lots of ideas. In fact, it was usually in the middle of the night that most ideas do flow into my mind. I'll be half awake half asleep. Those days there was rarely electricity so I won't be able to write down my ideas in the darkness. But then, I found out that I'll wake up in the morning and all the ideas that seemed vivid will disappear. One day, I was so frustrated as the poem I wrote in my head disappeared in the morning . My Mum advised me to begin to keep a pen and paper by my bedside and try to scribble anything I can on the paper. Then, when the idea comes, it would help me to actively remember it in the morning. I did that and it worked. My journey with writing began from that moment. My works were published in local magazine and church newspapers.

I was 17 and I had just finished my O level. We were waiting for our set results. I had planned my next move once my result comes out. I was certain of my result. I've always worked so hard and planned ahead, all while knowing my family situation at the time.

That morning, Mum casually came into our room (the room I shared with my two sisters). In her usual fond way, she said, "Chinma, you will go and learn how to sew at Da Dee's at Nkwogwu (our village market). Da Dee was a popular tailor in the village. He used to train women and men alike.

I was stunned as my mom pronounced the words. In fact, I was shocked that she could think in that direction. This is a woman who applied for me to take every and any entrance exam during my primary days knowing my abilities. Why would she want me to descend so low now?

She meant well. But I could sense defeat in her voice. Her eyes were in pain. I knew she could see where those words would take her beloved daughter. She didn't want any of that but she wanted to at least to offer her daughter something.

As a child who had always had big dreams, I could not see myself ending up in that little corner of a village of which I so much despise. With all my willpower, I said, "Mum, no!" "I will not."

As I said the words, I could hear her breath a sigh of relief. She did not utter a single word. She walked away relieved and proud again.

That willpower till today, renewed her hope, strength and mind. She knew from henceforth that, her daughter will never be defeated.

That strength of a child to refuse what was to box her in gave my Mum the determination to do all in her power never to deny us our God given purpose.

But then, life would beat and batter her. Every now and then those 'settle for less voice' would creep into her. Thankfully, she had already instilled in me the will not to settle.

So, we both would win each time.

Then, I stumbled onto Oprah Winfrey show. I fell in love with the woman I saw on TV, not quite sure at what age. I began to look out for her shows whenever possible. Then, when I was in school of nursing, I began to research more about her. I knew I wanted to be like her, in the sense of pursuing my dream of having my own media. That was the first encounter with wanting to create a media business.

Out of my Path

I had big dreams while growing up. Each time situation will present itself forcing me to lower my dream.

The temptations were often huge. I disagreed so much with Mum on issues of principles and deciding my fate. Sometimes it was inevitable to cave in.

When my grandmother died in 1995, just as I finished my WAEC(GCSE), I knew it was going to be a tough one for me to further my education. It was written all over the atmosphere. Times were hard when she was alive — let alone now that she is gone. I saw my Mum frequently feel defeated. We both passed the trial of becoming a tailor. I knew Mum was losing sleep about me. I cleared my WAEC with A – C and was within the top five best results in my school. I had prepared to go to uni to study Mass Communication, Media or Psychology.

I began to prepare for Jamb (entry exam to uni in Nigeria). I already knew the universities I wanted to attend.

It was barely 5am when Mum quietly came into my room. Everyone knew that it's something serious anytime Mum comes to our room with such demure at the wee hour. She sat down by my bedside and again called, "Chinma, listen my daughter. They situation is too tough and it's going to be hard for me to put you into university with all the corruptions there. I don't have money and no one to do the leg walk for me."

I was lost in my mind as she talked. What was Mum saying? Does it mean I won't go to uni? So what else will I be doing? I couldn't imagine myself dropping out of school. I had planned that within 30 years I would have had my PhD. So, in my mind, I knew all Mum was saying wasn't for me. I listened quietly as I fought the words as she spoke.

"So Mum, what does all you've said mean for me?" I questioned calmly.

Mum sighed heavily and said under her breath,

"Chinma, you will go to school of nursing."

"What?!!!" I screamed.

Mum continued to explain to me. She said, "I believe you will do well at school of nursing. You will gain admission and finish your studies on merit."

My entire life changed after that meeting. I began to fight for myself. I called my brother in Lagos, but he was as helpless as I was. He was trapped in working any job after seminary, as there was no money to pay for his uni to study accounting. He advised that I take the opportunity. At least it will help me get into higher education, even though it wasn't what I wanted. My uncles and aunties were of no help, as they all sanctioned my Mum's decision.

I began to pray about it. I also began to work with my Dad at his construction sites and got paid like any other labourer. I opened an account at a bank in my local market area. I began to save money for my jamb. We used to work from 9am to 6pm everyday. I would study for my jamb when I got home. I also continued to ask God of His own plan for me. I loved school; I never played with my education. In fact, there were times my only requests were to have my textbooks. During Christmas, I would beg Mum to only buy my books. I didn't need clothes or shoes.

So, I continued like that to prepare for my jamb. I registered for the jamb and took the exam. Unfortunately, I scored only 180, the general jamb cut off point at the time. While all the schools I chose had cut off from 200, my courses were even higher. I cried every night about my future.

Finally, I succumbed to Mum's decision on one term, being that it would be at the school of Nursing Owerri. I didn't want anything to do with the village. Then I went and applied to attend school of nursing. I chose only one school for all the three options.

I didn't want any chance of being posted to another school. That worried Mum a lot. Thankfully I passed very well and was taken.

While in school of nursing, I used to visit my friend at Imo State Uni. I would attend Mass Communication lectures with her. At some point, her classmates and lecturers thought I was one of them.

After nursing, I began my quest to study midwifery in the uni. I travelled from my village to Ibadan and Benin with my friend Amara. We registered in those universities for their Midwifery courses. Unfortunately, we were not taken. We made it at School of Midwifery Umuahia. I eventually settled with the fate of being a nurse/midwife.

One thing about me has always been to give my best in everything I get involved in. I was always at the top list of best students throughout my school of nursing.

My Why

You may see my drive through the lens of witnessing how black people are being bullied through negative media representation, which I saw when I arrived in the UK. That drive continues to make me look for ways to change the situation instead of blaming myself as I once did as a child. Every experience I've had has been worthwhile. I won't change a thing. Everything I want to do has been clear in my head and I've just been doing that. The abuse and bullying that I had faced helped me to spur to action whenever I notice the slightest of such on anyone.

While in school of nursing, there was my classmate who later became my best friend. She is still one of my closest friends, one of whom was being bullied because of her family background. ES has been telling us stories of how affluent her family was. With hindsight, I can see she was trying so hard to either belong or to cover up what was going on in her life. One fateful holiday, one of my classmates decided to pay her a visit unannounced. As soon as we came back to school, this girl opened the lid of almost a snapshot of the life which ES had tried so hard to conceal or paint out of her story.

Sometimes up to 10 or more of our classmates will gather talking about her, making jest of her. Everyone would start laughing and taunting her as soon as she appeared. She didn't quite know why that was happening. People were not talking to her or associating with her. She was alone. She would coldly sit at the corner of her bunk bed. She was often bemused, alone and looked dejected. She would retreat into herself, not able to speak to anyone as everyone were against her. Vibrant ES disappeared all of a sudden. I had to leap to her rescue as this bullying and taunting continued. I had to do something. I called one of my mates Obinma and told her how I felt about the ongoing bullying and gang up against ES. That day, we decided to do something. I and Obinma designed a hand drawn poster and pasted about three of different anti-bullying messages on the hostel walls. We also went further against every other person in the hostel, to become

ES's defence team. We would sit by her side, visit her corner after school, come in the morning to wait for her so we could go to class together. We watched out for anyone who said a word against her and we would take up the case.

We did this for a while until our mates got the message that we would not tolerate any form of bullying. Fortunately, I and Obinma were one of the brightest in our class and majority of the bullies truly do need us. So, they had to give up their bullying on our friend.

The story of our rescue mission with ES could be seen as my first clear steps towards my life mission which is to bring fairness, confidence and give people equal chance to thrive.

Someone asked me, "Why don't you merge the two events so you can have one big event?" I said to him, thank you but everything I do carries with it a very important message for specific people. It's not about the number or how large. Rather, it's about how relevant and how much I've been able to deliver that message. For example, the things that are said or done at Divas of Colour are clearly focused on empowering women of Colour, who are highly marginalised, abused and looked down on. The platform was created to help women of colour discover and embrace the many reasons they need to celebrate who they are, empower them to let the world know who they are and how they want to be seen, addressed and reached, as well as create the aura of self validation which ultimately helps to build confidence which is the first step towards self discovery. None of the activities at Divas of Colour can be tried at CA awards which is purely focused on promoting and adding value to the creativity and talent of African people, males and females. Different audience, different brand, different message and format too. Likewise, the same is true with our magazines.

My Ideals

I believe that everyone has something special to deliver to this world. Therefore, no one is more important than anyone else. I don't see myself more highly than anyone and don't see anyone more highly than myself. I respect everyone but do not fear anyone. I accord younger people the same respect I accord older people . One of my biggest traits is honesty. Sometimes people don't believe anyone can be so honest. I say it as I feel or know it. Also, I expect anyone dealing with me to tell me exactly what they mean. I believe that you mean what you say to me otherwise I will switch off from you. Sometimes it's weakness but most times it has been my strength.

I believe that everyone has once been young, but not everyone will live to be old. Whether you're old or young, there's something the next person knows that you will never know except you learn from them. If you look, then you will find.

I believe that if you're honest to yourself and do your part, then the universe will, in turn, give you all that you need to excel.

FAUSTINA ANYANWU

Making The Right Choices

I would like you to come with me. I'm telling my story so that you can find strength in yourself within your own situation. Sometimes we feel overwhelmed by what we see because we think we are alone. Hearing other people's stories can be a source of strength for you to start making a sense of your situation. Ultimately, people's own predicaments dictate what they think and feel about the world. These circumstances also come together to form their personality makeup. Each and every one of us form a defence mechanism on how to cope with whatever situation in which we found ourselves.

Situations offer us chances to have another look at who we are and who we are becoming. Paying close attention to the lessons in our situations will help us identify the different voices in our lives in which we should listen. As I grew up and began to leave home, there were many times peer pressure tried to push me into things which was not good. My voice of wisdom would come whispering. "Remember your Mum's suffering; how would she feel if she discovered you did that?" My Mum's face and voice followed me wherever I went. Her voice, her tears, and her pain was always present in my life. My every effort was to never add any more pain to her life but to make her proud. With these always on my mind, I didn't need any other awakening to know what to do at all times. I always weighed my choices against how it will affect my Mum's situation. That was my ultimate lifesaver, both in school and at everything else.

I took my time to study the things which I thought were wrong in my life and in my family. These things especially concerned my parents relationship. I took time to make varied comparisons of their marriage against other families I saw. From my empirical reasoning, I drew up a picture of how I wanted my own marriage to be. I knew nothing would change that. I made decisions that guided my decision in who to marry. I noted the traits I didn't want in my mind. They were my map. When I began to date, I avoided wealthy guys. I felt that they would be arrogant and would think they can buy me, just as they bought their latest Rolex. It was a put off if a guy showed off any affluence. I wanted a humble, purpose-driven guy who was confident in himself, owned his own story and was not running away from his weakness or background. You had to be superbly authentic to win me over.

SECTION TWO – POEMS

Introduction

I have decided to share some of my most-valued poems. They are a collection of my life's journey, expressed in the most honest way of which I could express them at the time. Each poem has been spontaneously written to tell a story of pain, healing and nostalgia.

Writing poems was my way of releasing and connecting with the right energy. These poems, just like every single word in this book, have been selected to be a source of empowerment for you. These poems are an eye opener to whatever you're going through. There will always be a way out; it might open a door waiting for you to come through.

The words in these poems always bring tears to my eyes, not that of pain but of triumph. The words make me laugh and give me direction in all I do.

I hope you will find them relevant, too.

TUNE IN

Dad Never Was There

It was so dark that night,
except the little light that shone from the moon.
Mum was crying, carrying the three of us;
the fourth still in the womb; due very soon
— maybe in a week more or less.

I remember my brother,
asking Mum what's the wrong.
Mum, still awkward, gave only a smile.
I was too young to understand what was wrong.
Never mind she said for, we will be fine.

The walk that night was strange to me.
Next, I remember we all sitting quiet
at the back of a van.
About nine or ten, we won't sleep yet.
How can I when I don't know what was wrong?

I keep wondering, in my mind,
where is Dad all this while.
Yet, each time I ask,
all I get is just a smile.
Though, I knew it's more of pain.

FAUSTINA ANYANWU

Grandma and Grandpa
Were there happy to care
for all of us — including Mum —
and the new baby, who is more dear.
Thanks to them for a while, no more pain.

Still, sometimes I ask
where is Dad all this while.
Why can't he help if he's alive?
All I ever get is just a smile
from the heart that burns in pain.

Thirty years or more later,
here I am but still not sure —
why is it my Dad can't even care?
I smile, just like Mum, yet I am not sure

How to heal all the wounds?

TUNE IN

We are Humans.

Sometimes we laugh.

Sometimes we cry.

Sometimes we walk.

Sometimes we fly.

We are humans.

Sometimes we curse.

Sometimes we pray.

Sometimes we work.

Sometimes we play.

We are humans.

Sometimes we win.

FAUSTINA ANYANWU

Sometimes we lose.

Sometimes we ask.

Sometimes we chose.

We are humans.

We task,
they tax.
We pay,
they play.
We watch them go.

We give,
they live.
We make,
and they take.
We watch them go; we watch them go.//

(Chorus)
We are humans,
we are humans....
We fade away,
in just one day.

TUNE IN

We bring,
they sing.
They eat our meat;
we watch them go.

We cry,
they fly.
We work,
They talk.
We watch them go; we watch them go.//

(repeat chorus.)

They laugh,
They bluff,
We die,
They lie,
We watch them go. We watch them go//

Note:

For the politicians, For the capitalist, For the lazy, For the busy, For the caring, For the workaholics..... We fade away in just one day.

I wrote this poem during the financial crisis of 2008, listening to politicians and so-called financial experts rattle words that made no meaning to the lives of everyday people. As a result, they inspired this poem. It reminds me how empty this world is. It was a moment that reminded me how important it was to value what we have now, – life!.

TUNE IN

All in My Heart

My eyes have seen enough
of all that the world can give.
Some written in my heart;
some on the walls.
Leaving with it traces
of disillusionment and regrets
Left by the very ones
To whom my life is trusted upon
How I hate to tell of the pain
How I wish to tell of the love
How I wish to be held
Even for once in the hand
By my Dad whom for all my life
I wait to hear him say
I love you.

Note:

I hope every parent will think twice of how their children feel before they jump in and out of marriage and relationships. How much it hurts can only be imagined. Every child longs to be loved by both parents. When I wrote this poem, I was in so much pain. In deep thoughts. Everything was not making sense to me, I couldn't take it any longer. I wished my dad could read my mind and make a change to the situation.

Most parts of life I have lived in situations where I had to defend myself, my mum, my family story. I have been embarrassed and confused. Growing up without my father's touch, love and care has been a big scar in my soul.

TUNE IN

My Little Girl

My little girl
When, when, when
will you go
to your bed and lay down?
Let it be tonight.
I'll switch off the light
and you sleep tight.

Note:

When I had my first child, I was faced with caring for a life without the help and guidance of my Mum. It was one of the toughest things I've ever had to face. Those sleepless nights made me realise even more how powerful my Mum had been. This experience brought me closer to my Mum and made me love and cherish her even more.

FAUSTINA ANYANWU

When I see your smiles.

When I see your smiles
Know my heart is filled with warmth
I could go for miles.

Note:

My marriage to my husband gave me a lot of healing. But the arrival of our girls were like icing on the cake. Looking at their faces and having to see those genuine smiles, open hearts, trust and loyalty always restored my faith in humanity.

In the words of Maya Angelou, "If you don't smile you die." A genuine smile brings lots of healing and bonding moments regardless of what type of relationship you share.

Every relationship needs a smile to survive. Keep smiling, for it's good for your heart, keeps you even younger than most anti-aging will do. When you smile at me, I could make another smile. On and on it goes.

TUNE IN

How About Now?

You loved me before
I loved you before
What ever happened to our love?
How about now...., how about now// (Chorus)

Baby come back where you belong
We've had it all together for long
We've gone to the moon
We've been to the desert
There's been times we had no one
We only got each other to love...

You loved me before
I loved you before
What ever happened to our love
How about now...., how about now// (Chorus)

Tell me right now my baby
What it is that turned you inwards
We've had our thoughts always forwards
Baby you know you can tell me anything
Whatever it is that's taking you away
You only belong here with me baby...

FAUSTINA ANYANWU

You loved me before
I loved you before
What ever happened to our love
How about now...., how about now// (Chorus)

Come back to me baby come back
Come back around, tell me you love me
Listen to my heart beat again
Don't let me go through this pain
All by myself in this lonely place
We have only now to be in love ....

You loved me before
I loved you before
What ever happened to our love
How about now...., how about now// (Chorus)

How about now... how about now// End.

Note:

I and my husband have always shared a very loving and caring relationship. But we had our first fight on this fateful day. It was devastating for me. It was never something I thought would happen. I was angry, bitter and ashamed. He was very bitter, angry and

TUNE IN

disappointed. The more we tried to blame the other for what was happening, the more we grew apart. That night I thought my marriage had hit the same rock as my Mum's. As I wrote this poem, I reminded myself the vow I made to myself, to my husband. I remembered the pain my Mum and shame my Mum would feel. I had to find a way to reach my husbands heart once again. I had to write him this poem, sneaked it into his side of the bed and we now live forever happily ever after.

FAUSTINA ANYANWU

I love you more

Baby you hold me
You kiss me
You love me
You made me who I am
And I will love you now
And I will love you forever
And I will love you more and more and more....

I was falling apart
Baby you got me back
You showed me light
In the darkest of night
You gave me life
When all doors shut in my face.

Baby you hold me
You kiss me
You love me
You made me who I am
And I will love you now
And I will love you forever
And I will love you more and more and more....

There were times

TUNE IN

I lost my cool
You held me in your arms
And whispered into my ears
The words that glued me back
Right back on my feet

Baby you hold me
You kiss me
You love me
You made me who I am
And I will love you now
And I will love you forever
And I will love you more and more and more....

At a time I was lost
So many demons after me
Baby you stood by me
Lifted me up away
From all that I feared
Now am living like human should

Baby you hold me
You kiss me
You love me
You made me who I am
And I will love you now

FAUSTINA ANYANWU

And I will love you forever
And I will love you more and more and more....

Tag: And I will love you now
And I will love you forever
And I will love you more and more and more....//(till fade).

Note:

My husband has been a God sent in my life. Through up and downs, at my lowest and my highest, he has always supportive. He never discards even my weirdest ideas. As someone who finds the best words to express my gratitude through poetry, I never miss the chance to let him know the deepest part of my heart.

TUNE IN

The Boy With The Hood

He's just a boy
full of life.
He loved his life.
He's just a teen
full of love and joy.
His eyes bright with stars
looking ahead with hope for the miles.
He's just a boy with the hood not a gun.

He lost it all in cold blood
for a sin he knew nothing about.
Just like everyone else he walked the street
only with skittles in his pocket not a gun.
Just like any other kid, full of life
he had his hood on, bought from the shops,
designed by a big name somewhere, famous and rich.
But, he's just a boy who had to die.

In cold blood he lost his life
for looking who he is and not who he ought to be.
In cold blood he lost his life
to a nation where he had every dream to live for.
In cold blood he lost his life
the dreams dashed and gone with it.

FAUSTINA ANYANWU

In cold blood he lost his life
to a law without regard for his life.

In cold blood he lost his life
and the law has a short hand to hold him up.
In cold blood he lost his life
like any other day, the world moves on.
In cold blood he lost his life
forever leaving his family empty and broken.
In cold blood he lost his life
because he's Black.
But Trayvon was just a boy with a hood over his head and not a gun.

Note:

I followed the case of Trayvon Martin and Zimmerman from the first day. And waking up to hear the verdict was the worst injustice I've ever heard. With so much pain in my heart and in solidarity with Trayvon's parents and the entire black race, I wrote this poem in tribute to the Boy who had to die so senselessly. If you're offended by this poem please flip by and do not comment .Thank you

TUNE IN

My Only Star

My only little star
Yes, my little star
One among so many
Now let everyone see
Light from your brightest beam
You oh my pretty little star
Stand above your many equals
Tall and with head held high
Arise with strength and vigour
Reach for the heights and shine through.

Note:

This was a poem of adulation for my first daughter Chelsea who was my joy and happiness at the time. Her beaming eyes and smiles never ceased to inspire and motivate me to appreciate my Mum, life and God.

FAUSTINA ANYANWU

They all say no

It's been rough.
It's been hard.
Everyone has let me down.
When I've come all so far
they look into my eyes and say no.
Why do people do what they do?
They all say no, no, no...
And I wonder....

(Chorus after each verse.)

They all say no
They all say no.
It's been lonely. It's been cold.
All I want is someone, a friend.
And they all say no...

I can see it in their eyes
though not a surprise
They're too busy, too fast living.
in a world that's too quickly moving.
When all I want is a friend,one to call mine

TUNE IN

so I don't have to be alone.
They all say no, no, no...
And I wonder..

My days are lonely, nights are long.
Where in this world do I belong?
They all say no, so where do I go?
In this world where they all say no.
Do I just wait, do I just go?
Where does my life belong?
They all say no, no, no..
And I wonder.

All I hear is no, all I see is no.. everywhere I go .., it's all no, I can feel it and I wonder... mmmmmmhhhhh......//

Note:

When we started our business, several times people ignored it. People snubbed it and didn't want to associate with us. At a point we were alone. We didn't have friends, nor did we have anything. Everybody we talked to for help or support would try to discourage us. It was one of the toughest experiences in my adult life.

FAUSTINA ANYANWU

One At A Time

One day at a time.
Says the traveler
on his way home,
or where he needs to go.

One sip at a time
says the old man
at the tea shop —
drinking, just to keep warm.

One step at a time
takes my little babe
learning for the first time
How to walk and dance.

One penny at a time
is not enough
to pay my bills
that come in ten pounds more at a time,
says the seller.

TUNE IN

So it's not my fault
if I had to charge ten times more
than what it's worth.
That's what the measurement gives.

Note:

The cost of living continues to rise every now and then. Why blame the others then, by trying by all means to make their life worthwhile? If there has to be peace everyone has a role to play. Inflation has ruined the peace of living. It's all about money after all.

FAUSTINA ANYANWU

The End is Nigh

Now there's sleep in my eye.
I can't even think.
Am about to sink.
I have to rest,
before I die.
I am so weak,
from my hurts.

Now it's ideal,
I get some warmth.
For today again is gone.
Not much for us,
is left to be done.
But to stay and wait
for our turn
to be with those
Who before us are gone.

Note:

My grandmother's death was and continues to be a big blow to everyone who knew her. She never allowed us to lack anything. After her death, life turned so badly that we did not have any place

TUNE IN

of hiding. This fateful day that I wrote this poem, I overworked myself. Getting home and feeling nostalgic, I began to reflect on how much death has rubbed humans of. In the end, all our struggles amount to the same fate.

FAUSTINA ANYANWU

Hello, New Year

Christmas has come and gone.
The memories becoming bygone.
We've had drinks we've had cake.
Some we bought some we 'bake'.
We've been out for the football.
This time there's no snowball,
to throw about, yet we had fun.
Though the other side had won.
So we await to bid thee.
Helloooo.

The boxes are all now opened.
The packs are all flattened.
Some gifts wanted, some not.
Some adorned, another with fault.
All friends have now left.
And no one has reported any theft
at least until this moment.
If any, my family will be blunt.
So we await to bid thee.
Helloooo.

TUNE IN

The table is set, champagne ready
while we sit watching 'Ugly Betty'
blab and blab of her holiday.
Everyone glancing at the clock in dismay.
As the tick and the tuck
seems to move only by luck.
Then, the horns begin to rave.
With more drinks ,no time to behave.
So we sing to celebrate thee.
Helloooo.

Note:

We all look forward to every new year with such excitement. The optimism is such a beautiful thing to behold.

FAUSTINA ANYANWU

The Great Britain.

The brave warrior.
The pride of Europe.
The master of many nations.
I do hail thee.

You never fail to fight for man.
Where others fear to go
there do you tread.
You are fearless.

You open your shores
for the sake of the oppressed.
A leader by example.
A great host.

Only you Britain
could speak the language
that connects all.
You are indeed great.

TUNE IN

Note:

Looking at the history of Great Britain, regardless of what you think, hear or say about this nation, you can attest to their history of greatness. As little as this nation may seem, they somehow managed to get over half of the world to speak their language and to adopt their culture. Not forgetting their woes and negative impacts, in this poem, I deliberately chose to bring s side of the nation which unfortunately, this generation may only have to imagine how great their nation once was.

FAUSTINA ANYANWU

The Morning Breeze.

Stretch out your hands.
Feel the morning breeze.
Let the gentle blow,
caress your mind.
Fill your heart with joy.
For once let the world be.

Open up your soul.
Lay bare your mind.
Let the cool air,
blow away this emptiness.
Fill the gaps with peace.
For once let the world be.

Widen your ears.
Listen to the sound
of the early morn breeze.
Fill your heart with the rhythm
and softness of its vibe.
For once let the world be.

Lay bare your mind.
And drift off to sleep.

TUNE IN

Let the world for once be.
Let the cool gentle breeze
take you back to sleep.
For once let the world be.

Note:

When I turned 30, I struggled a lot to come to terms with my reality. Having come to Uk and not being able to achieve my set goals at the time was a huge knock for me. I soon realised I was going through midlife crisis. Empowered from reading lots of books, I began to come to terms with my life and started building towards my life purpose. This night I woke up to talk to myself to calm down for once and let the world be.

TUNE IN

My Mother

Who is she that carried me,

for nine good months, in her womb,

to make sure I survive this earthly life?

My mother.

Note:

Her name is resilience.
Her name is power.
Her name is grace.
And she is my mother.
My mother has been a vessel of greatness and God has continued to be her announcer.
Mothers are eternal and must be cherished. How often do you celebrate your mother?

FAUSTINA ANYANWU

I Don't Want to Talk

Now take your case
to the wall.
Let silence
be the judge.
for you and I.
For tonight
my mouth will never
let open
to spit even a word.

TUNE IN

Note

Marriage is a very interesting adventure. It will teach you, build you and have you matured. On this fateful night I've had a major fall out with my husband. I was hurt and bruised. But maturity and experience taught me to cork up my words. And it so worked.

Sometimes we want to talk and get back at our opposition. We want to shout out our right and fight. But sometimes, silence is all that is needed to calm the roaring storm. Patience and self control are the only virtues you will need to be in control in life's most troubling times.

Remember, your words have the power to create or destroy. If those words are not going to heal then keep them with you. Silence can be golden.

FAUSTINA ANYANWU

You have a choice

If I had to walk.
Then I will walk.
Today came with its plan.
I keep running.
I keep moving.
Not because I want to
but I just have to.

Just like now
I don't have the time
to check the rhyme,
the rhythm and flow
of what I'm writing.
I just have to keep writing
as it comes to my mind.

If I don't, I guess I will lose it all.
Not that I want to.
But I reckon I have no time to…
To wait around thinking.
You know some days are like that.
They keep passing
and we keep living.

TUNE IN

If you don't, you had miss so much.
At least that's what we've been made to believe.
But then you can stop and think.
Yet, again if you have the time.
Like me I don't have the time.
Fast and quick and in a haste.
I wish you too can just read
this as quickly as you can.

But wait.
If you can have the courage
to steal the time to stop and think,
you had know this is life after all.
We don't really have the time to think
to figure things out.

With that,
Then I decided no, it's my choice.
Yes, it's my choice to decide what I write
just like you it's your choice to live
how you want to live.
Fast, quick and in a haste.
Slow, slow and slow.
You have to choose.
You alone have the power to choose.

FAUSTINA ANYANWU

Come to think of it,
we actually do have a choice.
For that I decided,
it's time for me to stop.
It's my choice.

Note:

This is a thought rather than a poem. It's totally a free verse and requires you to get into it to really appreciate it. The world is full of people and things that are ever ready to disapprove of you. We're often made to feel and think we have no choice but to continue to follow the same old theories and laid down foundations. When is actually fact, you can only be able to unleash your creativity when you exercise your power of choice.

TUNE IN

It's just a Dream

Suddenly I saw my wings
grow wide and thick and sparkly.
I could fly up to the sky.
I saw the moon, I touched the stars
and I could walk the cloud.
A beautiful sight to see.

I built my house up the sky.
I rugged the rooms with the cloud.
I shared a walkway with the moon,
and the stars were my friends.
I looked to my left and looked to my right,
I looked to the front and looked to my back.

I nodded to myself,
This is where I belong.

Suddenly,
I woke to see it was just but a dream.
But I said to myself,
If I could just dream it,
then it can come to pass.
So I made up my mind that it was real.
Then I looked to see, I still had my wings.

FAUSTINA ANYANWU

Note:

Sometimes it could just be a dream. But what is wrong to have a big dream? If I can even imagine it then It can come true .

I have not used any form that is none to anyone. As always I choose to do it as it is – Like myself. It is my choice what I call a poem.

I hope you enjoy it and make sense out of it.

TUNE IN

For all that you gave me

You gave me not just food to eat.
You gave me a part of you to live.
You said not just the words for me to hear.
You gave me the mind to think for myself.
You showed me not just what to do.
You gave me hands that I may do it myself.
Now Mum for all that you gave to me,
It's my turn to give you all that I am.

Note

Happy mother's day. To every Mum who has been a true mother.

FAUSTINA ANYANWU

The Sojourners' Dialogue.

The breeze of life is short.
The life of growth is ageless.
A heart of love is deep.

Where the heart of love dwells
peace and trust are deeper than wells.

See the snows are white but never pure
compared to the purity of a heart so true.

The snow is whiter
but the heart is brighter.

Beauty, white and bright
purity remains most true.

White and purity.
Bright and Beauty.
All are gifts from He full of wisdom.

TUNE IN

Are these gifts to be given or reserved?
Or must they be conserved and preserved?

Those who have eyes to see it.
Those who know it when they see it.
Must these gifts be shown.

No! The gifts are shown to all
God lets his rain pour on all
good, bad or wicked.
He redeemed and loved us all
even when He was rejected.

He came to redeem and save
those who yawn for freedom as slaves.
He humbled himself to become one with us
in all things except in sin.

With eyes of love
we look up above
to him without sin.

FAUSTINA ANYANWU

In him we place our hope
when we stand on rope.

Oh! that I may reap from the ripe trees,
and laugh myself to a lively sleepy sleep.

And for once my heart let the world be
as I sleep my heart and soul
to the sweet sounds from birds and bees.

How would the world be?
Does the heart hear?
No! Let the heart heat the cold world.
And the world wear the torn heart.

Tear not a heart as silent as a babe
and as peaceful as the dove
for my heart cherish but only love.

Tear and wear

TUNE IN

*so that you may
mend and tear no more.*

*May I never wear a torn heart
for to tear and mend
will only leave on a scar.*

*A scar is a symbol of history
evoking the past
for one who has a past.
Teaching and telling what to never do,
reminding us where we come from
and where we are going to.*

*Where we are going,
only but love
patience and persistence
can take us.*

*Godspeed to the fair passenger.
Sweet dreams to the dreamer.
Well done to the hard worker.*

FAUSTINA ANYANWU

*Till journey, dream, and hard work embrace,
then shall we fly to our destination.*

Amen!!!

Note:

The Sojourner's dialogue depicts a life journey. In this case, 3 friends on a life voyage to an unknown land. They are filled with despair and uncertainty. As they navigate their way through life, they are questioning and reflecting on all they have been told, all they have learnt, heard and experienced. There were moments of disbelieve and confusion. At each time when the voice of defeat shows up, the voice of encouragement, and victory comes back to comfort and pull them through. Just like in our lives. We are in a journey. Sometimes we are disillusioned by what we see, heard, and experience. In these moments, God's voice continues to speak words of courage and comfort to us. The important things often is to listen carefully to that gentle voice which explains it all to us.

TUNE IN

Summer

Up there is the sky
For those who fly high
Bright and white and blue
Home for the stars and moon
A place for the sun to bloom
With radiance we hope for soon
When summer comes taking the gloom
Heaped on us from the cold winter's doom.

FAUSTINA ANYANWU

Will

Where we are going
Road and machine mean nothing
Determination,
Self-will and motivation
Will get us on and moving.

TUNE IN

They Will Never See

At the beginning of everything

ever is,

many will look, not understanding

what there is.

Some will look but do not want to see.

What's to be.

Others will look again and again.

But don't have power to gain,

insight to what's to become.

Note:

Whenever we declare ourselves and begin to pursue our life purpose, it is always those closest to us who disregard us, doubt us and discourage us.

FAUSTINA ANYANWU

The Refugee

Oh what a very long lonely journey
to such a very short busy distance.
In this very terribly strange instance
there's no time to have even a brief dance
with the weather so awfully angry.
Especially in this cold unknown land.
It has been worthwhile though, all the way through.
At least the fun of finding our heros,
has kept the mind away from the sorrow
engraved on by a war trodden homeland.
But if over and over you asked me,
I wish I'd not taken the route again.
Who wouldn't now want to go it easy?
Knowing we were insane with so much pain.

You never know what else life may bring.
I wish it could be easy all the same.
Honestly, you don't have to take to blame.
Don't blame me for I saw pain when I came.
My dear, there's no prize for the suffering.
At least that is what I heard elders say.
Never mind whatever that saying meant.
For a moment, I had it in my thought.
By the way, what's even more important?

TUNE IN

Is it the lessons learnt this very day?
Or do one stick his miserable mind,
Only on things so awfully angry?
Or is it better to try and unwind,
from the stress of a very long journey?

Note:

If we can step out of our own self to see the plight of refugees then we can appreciate the horror facing humanity. Pains of people fleeing their homeland because of war, famine and displacements should make us show compassion and not disdain. For if these people had a choice, they wouldn't want to risk their own lives, leave their own home, property, achievements and a familiar life. But they had to keep the hope alive, hope that on the other end they could find the face of humanity.

This poem is dedicated especially to the migrants who have lost their lives and freedom crossing the mediterranean looking for the face of humanity but was rather met with brutality of man.

FAUSTINA ANYANWU

The Beauty of Nature

Behind the bare winter trees,
the early morn' moonlight shines.
So is the beauty of life,
reserved for a few to find.
How lucky to be with those,
chosen to see the beauty,
of the hand work of He full of wisdom.

At the tip of stems of thorns,
the beautiful red rose buds.
A measure to keep it from,
the prying eyes of the fools.
How lucky to be with those,
chosen to see the beauty
of the hand work of He full of wisdom.

Note:

Sometimes we are swamped by the struggles of life that we fail to stop and enjoy the beauty around us, the beauty of nature. Nature, is such a beauty to behold if we can for once step out of our artificial world of worry, status, ambition and fight for survival.

TUNE IN

God

God?

she asked.

Do you believe there's one?

She did her best to convince me.

But I can't go with you.

Not in that direction, I said.

Well,

I was not there at the beginning

so it's not for me to prove

the story of creation.

But I have seen the beauty of His works,

the arrangements, events, the sequence.

FAUSTINA ANYANWU

Day by day it shows

and I can't just help my dear, but to believe.

There must be someone, somewhere in charge.

The supervisor, the manager,

the owner of this wonderous world.

Call him whatever you wish.

I chose to call him God — THE SUPREME.

Note:

As a firm believer in God, I see everyday and in everything the hand of God. His grace has been sufficient for me. He never ceases to pleasantly surprise me at the time when you think there is no way out. Each day of my life as I go, He confirms His omnipresence in my life.

TUNE IN

Pundiyaya

These three birds,
came on my window,
All whisper to my ears.
Pundiyaya.

I heard them say,
the favoured one.
Have a nice day.
Pundiyaya.

I think they are angels,
with a message of hope
From my window angles.
Pundiyaya.

Each have green marks,
I think they're beautiful.
Shiny wings, beaks that sparks.
Pundiyaya.

Note:

I was reflecting on our situation at the time, worried and filled with fear for the feature. Suddenly, these three birds showed up on the window and these words came to me. And immediately I felt this peace within. Inspired by the scene I could interpret the word Pundiyaya as peace. Totally new word, never heard it or know if it's any language at all. I would say, then Pundiyaya is my invented word.

As you read this beautiful work of imagination, I wish you pundiyaya.

TUNE IN

It's Winter Again

The leaves are gone.
The trees are bare.
The house is cold and damp.
The streets are filt and messed
The dog walker lets them foul,
Here and there.
It's winter again.

The cold is back.
The coats are out.
The days are dark.
The nights are long and chilled.
The bus is stuffed and filled
Windows tightly locked.
It's winter again.

The cold is freezing.
They all walk like duckling
All wrapped in just the same colours
Black, brown and gray.
And no smiles on anyone's face.
It's winter again.

Note:

Having lived in such tropical country as Nigeria, experiencing winter for the first time was such a challenge. One of the most dreaded times for me as I still find it difficult to cope with the cold, the mess, the heater, the smell and face of it. But then, it is these differences that make the memories we share once we're back with loved ones at home in Nigeria.

TUNE IN

A Soldier's Day To Love.

This is not a day

to live far away.

For now is the time

to make you mine.

For I have only tonight

to hold you tight

in my arms, close to my chest

away from the gaze of the rest.

Note:

2014, as the surviving soldiers arrived after the Afghan war where hundreds of British soldiers lost their lives, I watched with tears in my eyes as families of these soldiers came face to face with their husbands, wives, parents, sons and daughters. Some of the soldiers met their babies for the first time. Emotions were rising, you could feel the pains and joys and confusion in the faces of all, those who had lost their wards and those who were lucky to have theirs back alive.

TUNE IN

Lord, you are good

For whatever we are doing.
We do with love.
For whatever we are seeing.
We see your face.
For whatever we are hearing.
We hear your voice.
For Wherever we are going
We come to you.
Lord, for you are good.
For you are Love.

SECTION THREE – QUOTES FOR SUCCESS

Note:

All quotes in this book are all my original quotes and must at all times be attributed to me.

TUNE IN

Experiencing Success

"When the zeal to succeed exceeds the fear to fail, only then can you begin to experience the sweet taste of success."

Self Belief

"Believing in myself does not mean I know it all. Rather, it means I know I can get better and am trying."

The law of giving

"Giving more than I take challenges me to make more than I have."

Be Persistent

"Keep doing till you achieve as long as you are still alive."

FAUSTINA ANYANWU

Parenting

"Give your child the best,

Of your youth.

At old age,

You will know rest."

Secure your space

"Hold your heart very closely and your mind very carefully. You will need both intact if you must succeed."

"Beware of those who crowd over your growth. It's like a maize growing under a mango tree. The shade will not allow it to get any Sun for it to germinate."

TUNE IN

"You fall into your own ditch if you continue to chase your competitor. Set your goals and crush them. Focus on your goals = your success."

"While they're busy chasing the famous we are busy becoming more relevant and sooner or later they will be chasing us."

"You must draw your business lines. If you don't, you will never know when those lines have been crossed."

"Remember never to make your business decisions personal. Although personal biases may sometimes play a role."

FAUSTINA ANYANWU

"Connect with those who understand where you're going and are willing to go with you or help you get there."

"In business, you must be prepared to learn from others. It's best to listen to and learn from newcomers in your industry even. They have a wealth of new ideas and knowledge. They are more current with new developments and tricks. And they are not yet so keen for money as this time, they are only interested to know that people are listening. Unfortunately, many people are too proud and are stuck with how many years they've been doing the same things."

TUNE IN

"Listen to everyone. But, be sure what you want to decide. At the end of the day, you alone will live with the consequences of the choices that you make."

"It doesn't matter how long you've been in an industry, if you're not upgrading your knowledge, then you expire. Simple!"

"Whatever you seek from social media you will get just as whatever you want out of life you will get."

"Anyone ready to stand up does not make excuses or play the blame games."

"Running a business is a different kind of school. The exams will never finish. You will pass some and fail some. You never graduate, therefore you must keep learning."

"In your journey, you will hear and see a lot. All are there to teach and prepare you for the next turn you're going to take."

"In your journey, you're going to meet so many. A lot will betray you and leave you hanging out there to dry. But, you will have a few holding you up. Cherish these few and let the many go."

TUNE IN

"It's important that you know you're in this journey for the legacy and not for the chase. You must keep walking and keep leaving those footprints. They will be your evidence that you came and you did your best."

"Let your footprints do the talking. That is what authenticity does. Legacy."

"Embrace the journey as you find your destination."

"It's never for the money you see, it's about the impact and living the dream. It's always about adding value and money will find its way in."

"To make the most of it, my social media became a case of DDA (Develop, Discover and Action). Develop the message, Discover who needs it and take action selling your message. It's that simple."

"Be most wary of those who pinch on your self confidence."

"Being strong isn't about how much you can carry in your heart. It's about how much you're willing to off load. It's about finding yourself and living while still alive. It's about admitting your weaknesses and working to improve. It is not about how fast you can put another human down, but how much you can build yourself and others up."

TUNE IN

"It is about knowing when to stop and ask for help. It is about giving and accepting help when needed. It is about doing your best and leaving the rest."

"We don't need weightlifters to change the world. All we need are people being great at the little things they do. You and I knowing we could be great from our little contributions."

"Some doors seem closed because you've not known how to turn the knob."

FAUSTINA ANYANWU

"Since I stopped being strong and started being me, I've suddenly become stronger."

"In the pursuit of your excellence remember you do not always have to do anything physically. You can immerse yourself in meditation to energise your spirit where all energy come from."

"If you keep your head up, the world will see your face."

"The only way to see up is by looking up."

"Humility brought me here and I'm prepared to follow her wherever she takes me."

TUNE IN

"Discover yourself, when you do, love her so much that you will never have any reason not to be her."

"If no one counts you, then count yourself."

"Confidence is never measured by how loud or noisy you can be. Know when, where and how to use your voice."

"Do all you can when you can, for the time will come when you can't."

"The wisdom you seek is always in the page you never opened."

"Your voice may not be loud enough. But, the songs that you sing will last forever. Always sing your best."

"You will never know the joy of sowing until you take that action."

"When negative and twisted people want to infiltrate your space, block them off with silence. Save your energy for something more important."

"When you give the world all that is in you, the world in turn gives you all that you need."

TUNE IN

"When you begin to live your life like nobody is watching, then you begin to soar like an eagle."

"You don't have to prove yourself if you are being yourself."

"If you keep your hands clean, gold will stay on them."

"Walk away whenever in doubt; keep walking."

"I will have to be myself again if I have to be anyone. Make it a point to be real with who you are."

FAUSTINA ANYANWU

"If you can keep the enthusiasm, then you will reach the summit."

"If you haven't been there, never judge those who are there. There are things only experience can teach."

"One person willing to cruise with you is enough to set the sail."

"There's so much space in the world to accommodate all and more. Why squash in a corner? Find your space and cruise your ship there."

TUNE IN

"At first, it's the people who know you that will doubt your ability. However, once you've got strangers believing in you, know that you're set for success."

"Don't be deceived. You need media coverage to stay relevant and to create your brand awareness."

"It's never who started first. It's all about who endures to the end."

"No one can defeat a person who never gives up."

"There isn't much you can do to please someone who isn't pleased with you. The few who appreciate you will always be pleased with your efforts."

"Love yourself so much that nothing can put you down."

"If you're never grateful for what you have, then you will never see the value it holds."

"For every puzzle you only need to find one missing piece and it's game over."

TUNE IN

"Who are these people?
They're not happy enough to be happy
with you or for you.
They're not compassionate enough to empathise
or feel your pain.
They're not rich enough to see your value.
They're not humble enough to ask for your help.
They're not big enough to impact your life.
They don't have time to spend with you
They demand for your favours so arrogantly as if
it's their birthright.
Whoever they are, you do not need
them in your space."

FAUSTINA ANYANWU

"Since I chose to be happy,
to smile,
to forgive,
to be different,
to live
and to be just me.
All my weaknesses have suddenly
become my strength."

"While they're busy chasing the famous, we're busy becoming more relevant and they will soon begin to chase us too."

TUNE IN

"The answer is always in the rhythm.
If you listen carefully, then you will hear.
The answer is always in the sound.
If you listen carefully you will hear it."

"Overconfidence and underconfidence are both dangerous.
Check that you're not on either side of the spectrum."

"Being a CEO means you must walk your brand to success.
Talk is cheap but action is priceless."

FAUSTINA ANYANWU

"The most valuable investment you will make in your life is surrounding yourself with people who will show you the way. I will pay anything to have them around me."

"You cannot be everything to everyone. But, you can be you to yourself."

"My biggest problem is that I see through people's lies and can't pretend I didn't catch them out."

"Hold your heart very closely and your mind very carefully. You will need both intact if you must succeed."

TUNE IN

"Listen to everyone. But, be sure what you want to decide. At the end of the day, you alone will live with the choices that you make."

"You will hear and see a lot. All are there to teach and prepare you for the next turn you're going to take."

"In your journey, you're going to meet so many. A lot will betray you and leave you hanging. But you will have a few holding you up. Cherish these few and let the many go."

SECTION FOUR – THOUGHTS ON SUCCESS

TUNE IN

Finding Success.

I've always had the thought to have my own media business for as long as I can remember. This thought was inspired from when I encountered Oprah Winfrey, who continues to be my icon and secret mentor. I used to imagine and see myself as an executive of a big media business. I held on to those, regardless of what life brought my way. I believed and knew that one day it will happen.

Then came the reality of hard times directing me away from that vision. But, I still held on to it. Most times I secretly had it. I had to even hid the thought of becoming a successful media entrepreneur from my own mind. Even your own mind, at times, plays up the idea that it can't be done. The first and most important part of succeeding is to calm that little voice within you. Your ability to step out towards your dream is to first convince that little voice that continually doubts your ability. It continually reminds you of all the reasons why you can't succeed in what you set out to do. You must keep it under control and flood it will the right answers. In my case, I had to carefully keep the discussion away from that little voice. I refused to have that chat with it.

I realised any time I attempted to have that discussion, this little voice told me, "Look how much you've had to suffer. Even your Mum who had everything — the money, the family support — and still everything failed. How much more you will you carry all the baggages? You better not try because you already know the answer. It shows me all the people who have tried and failed. How do you think you can make it on your own? Besides, where will you find the initial capital in which to begin?"

The little voice could be so strong. The fear it brings is so powerful that you become paralysed. Until I made a conscious decision to keep it out of the discussion. At this time, It seemed as if the idea had been dropped and that little voice became happy. I deceived it.

Dropping her from the discussion gave me opportunity to discover something much stronger. I stopped thinking and started taking one step action everyday towards realising my dreams, regardless of what life brings. It didn't matter how small. I began to read. I made a goal to read every and anything that can be read. Reading opened a whole new world for me. It took me through many places and brought me face to face with people who have been in much worse situations and made it out greater. Reading made me realise I have been dwelling in self-pity all this time. I realised my life hadn't been that bad after all.

Reading became my first saving grace. I made friends with so many successful people. First, I began to study about women I have always admired: Oprah Winfrey, Maya Angelou, Alicia Keys, and later, Michelle Obama. And I as I dug into these women, I discovered something. They all were born in January just like me. And they all had another thing in common. They had all gone through a tough period to come out on top. These exposures began to open up a new brand of me who was fearless, hopeful and eager to win.

I began to blog. I saw my blog as the next big thing. I gave it my all. I poured my heart into it. I made sure I researched every article I wrote. As I wrote, my confidence began to grow stronger. Something happened as my blog grew. I discovered there were so many other women like me out there running their small businesses who didn't have a voice. They were yawning to be heard and seen. They needed to be encouraged by telling their stories. My mind opened as I discovered this; I could see my moment show up.

I became a happier person as I discovered myself and saw the possibility in my journey. My life completely changed from a place of pity and defensiveness to a woman open to possibilities. I stopped seeing all the limitations and excuses. This was a moment in my life that I cherished so much. I now make every effort to always dwell in it. I always start all over everyday. I make an effort to keep the momentum and motivation, as well as staying self-driven. It has to be new everyday of the journey. I have to continue to see the picture which I saw at the beginning. I have to keep seeing possibilities in everything.

I discovered something else as this continued. The more I worked towards my vision, the more doors began to open. This leads to the passage of my purpose. I could see the proverbial light at the end of the tunnel.

But wait! What I didn't know was that, that light at the end of the tunnel was that far. This was a good thing.

Lesson:

Be your own leader. It doesn't matter who is expecting what from you or however well-intended they might be. If you want to make the most of your life and actualise your dream, then you must detach yourself from their expectations of you and become your own leader.

- You must take control of your own life.
- Make your own decisions. Face it and take responsibility for the outcomes of your decisions.
- Believe in yourself. You must start believing in those 'little ideas' of which you've always talked yourself out of doing.
- You must stop believing in those negative talks that you've heard all your childhood; all the 'you cannot statements.'
- You must move away from those negative habits— both those learnt from your home and from friends. Those become limiting habits, so you must learn to drop them. Most people don't succeed because of their parents. They never allow you to explore life or to discover yourself. You must cut off from their own fears packaged as love.

My Mum was such a wrap up for me as a child. She cast all her fears over me since I was the first daughter. She wanted the best for me, therefore letting her fears of allowing me to make mistakes took over her ability to allow me to develop. She guided all my steps. I fought so hard to let myself out of her hold. Even when I knew very well what I was doing and what I wanted, my Mum within her always thought I was still a child that needed guidance. That caused a lot of rebellion and fight between us. When I finally got into school of nursing, Mum introduced me to several distant relatives who lived in the city, to take care of me. Yet, if I fail to come home any weekend, Mum will show up in my school the next Monday morning. It became a ritual even my classmates and lecturers became acquainted with over time.. My Mum would come to my school, takes me to the shop to buy my provision, body lotion, soap, even undies. Till today, I still struggle with buying my undies.If I do, I will get the wrong size.

Sometimes I used to worry how I would live without my Mum.

At the age of 20, I got admission to study midwifery at Umuahia. My Mum began the same ritual. She would come to my school every week to help me do my shopping. We didn't have much free time to go home while I studied midwifery, so she had to come. One day, I decided enough was enough. I told Mum to give me the money for my shopping that I would go myself to the market. But, she refused and I stood my ground. That was my first day of pulling myself out of my Mum's hold of fears. She also refused to allow me. I had to stand on my feet. I told her I didn't need the items if she wouldn't want to let me do my own shopping. I refused to go with her and she left with her money. She thought I would change my mind and come home in few days. I didn't have anything on me at school. But to her dismay, I stayed another two weeks and didn't come home. She finally came back at the beginning of the third week, bringing a few things and left me with some money to take care of other things I needed. That was the day of my liberation.

Build the skills.

Forming the habit of reading for a purpose was the greatest life structuring thing I did. I could hear the authors; they were my life coaches. Autobiographies were my best friends. I discovered that motivation alone cannot take you that far. I needed the skills to take me through. I began to learn. I enrolled for journalism courses, I would go for conferences and workshops. I searched for free ones and I searched for affordable ones. I also learnt to offer my services in exchange for what I needed. As I grew, I realised that as much as you need the technical skills, you also need the business skills, such as: negotiation skills, managerial skills, and many other things to run a business. I was eager and ready to learn. One of the best gifts God gave me is the ability to learn anything very quickly. I knew this ever since but this time, I had to test it for my own self deliberate purpose. I began to teach myself a lot. I taught myself design skills and anything you could imagine. Books and the internet continued to be my best school.

My dogged determination to find my way led me to lots of amazing breakthroughs. It opened even more doors, leading me to places I never imagined. From giving it my all, I discovered we could publish magazines. The possibilities are endless and there were no obstacles.

The Power Of Mentorship

One of the greatest challenges facing this generation is the get-rich-quick attitude. People no longer want to go through the process. They want to get paid hugely with no valid portfolio. Everybody needs a mentor, a role model or a teacher. Someone who would hold your hand and is willing to guide you. You also need to be willing and humble to learn from their own experiences. The process of mentorship could be formal or informal.

In the past, it used to be called apprenticeship. People formally enroll to learn the skills about the world and about their own ability. A period of apprenticeship helped people to understand the trade and build confidence in their ability.

Unfortunately, these days it's difficult to find an honest mentor who is willing to teach and give the best guidance to the mentee. Most mentors are afraid that their ward will overtake them in the constant competitive internet make believe world of new 'entrepreneurship' mind-set. Also, most younger generation of people are finding it hard to keep their head down to learn and go through the process. They are fixated on being paid cash instead of learning how to make and keep the cash.

When we started, there was a lady I looked up to in practical terms. I learnt a lot from her. I was happy to follow her, tell her my next plan and run the idea with her. Her opinion was honestly received. I made sure I was at every of her events and made sure she was updated on what I was doing. Her platform was a great eye opener for me. We were like big sister and little sister. Everything went well until she began to feel threatened by my progress. A few things happened and she began to block me. I would tell her about some of my projects in the pipeline; then, she and her husband would run to start it first. She stopped giving me opportunities. She would actually block any from any meaningful contact I made her to know about. I watched this happen several times and as soon as I was convinced of what was going on, I confronted her. Of course, she denied it and tried to cover her back. But the sequence continued, I had to pull out. I still respect her till today as she was a great guidance through the beginning.

Regardless of what happens, never underestimate the power of mentorship. It doesn't matter how many books you read or lessons you attend. You need a practical guidance. Someone who has done it before can show you some of the pitfalls. They can introduce you into the industry and the relevant networks, people and trends. Someone would help you navigate the policies and laws. Someone who will applaud you for the small wins and one that would be honest and constructively tell you where you got it wrong. If you're lucky to find one person who can do this, make the most of it while it lasts.

TUNE IN

Expect the Challenges.

The ride to success is not a smooth one. Which is why keeping your WHY at the forefront is very important. This is why you must hold on to the euphoria of self-discovery. This is why you must be highly confident and be your own biggest fan.

When I began my blog in 2011, my baby was just about three months old. My Mum visited from Nigeria. She was a great help and also was going to be a stumbling block. Her love — or do I say her show of love — was becoming a hinderance. She would remind me how long I have spent on the computer working. I used to spend almost all my nights in front of my computer. That was the only time I could work effectively. In the night, my three daughters, all toddlers, would be well asleep. I could do my research, learn and blog. My Mum was filled with so much pity for me. Her daughter was taking too much in her perspective. She thought I was suffering myself. Sometimes, she would say, "Chinma, you're suffering yourself too much. You're still breastfeeding and you're keeping late night; what kind of money is this you're chasing?"

I looked at my Mum with such pity after having read books and seeing myself in a different place. She didn't know what I was doing and I didn't expect her to know either. I would ignore her. I knew the drive was something more than money. It was never about money. If it was, I could easily go back to being a nurse and earning a 'decent salary' enough to get us things that we needed and wanted.

If dealing with my Mum's fears was tough enough then wait for the real deal. It wasn't long before my Mum left and I was faced with the kids alone. And I had to put in practise all that I have been learning. Time structuring, effectiveness, resource management was all important. My husband had to go to work to keep us going. It wasn't long until that new adventure was eating much deeper than we expected into the family finances. Gradually, money became a tough stone to crack. The more we did, the more money we needed to put into the business. Still there was nothing turning in from the business.

I remember once when it became so hard for us to keep up with the financial obligation of running a business. Putting food on the table became a huge task. Each day that comes makes it clearer that we can't continue. Yet, we were convinced that this is what we want to do. We were convinced that our idea was a great and needed one. We just had to find the right way to get the message across and continue to build our readership and gain loyalty.

I began to make roasted peanuts and Chin-chin (a Nigerian snack). At first, I didn't know how to make them; I tried anyway. I took the first sets to a local grocery shop and they took stock. That encouraged me to try more. With a few weeks I became popular with the local grocers around. I began to receive calls to supply more peanuts. My peanuts were selling very fast and shops were making much margin. I was regularly told that it was fresh and different. As I did this, the shop owners continued to give me feedback on what to do, how to package and which packaging and price sold better.

TUNE IN

Some of them helped me source better and cheapest suppliers for all I needed. At a time, I wasn't able to keep up with the demand. Even as this side business grew, I knew it wasn't what I wanted and would not allow it to distract me from my purpose. This peanut business helped us to stabilise a little with running our magazine business. We began to have enough money to do the necessary budgeting for marketing and other things.

Lesson:

1. Challenges are opportunities for you to discover another opportunity and skill within.
2. It is a channel of training and testing your why. When your why is feeble, you can easily get distracted and pulled away from the purpose.
3. It is another opportunity to re-evaluate your why and your life.
4. Challenge helps you build your character.
5. It stripes you of unnecessary associations helping you to stay focused.
6. You learn to be more resourceful. Learn to appreciate what you have and who you are.

SECTION FIVE – ENTREPRENEURSHIP

TUNE IN

No need to fear

My greatest fear is, not being able to do what I want to do.

There are several things that we can be scared of in our lives. These things are not what really gives us the fear. Rather, we simply are just afraid of our own selves. Fear resonates from what we feel rather than what we know. I have always pondered on this subject for the most of my life. I realised that I don't really have any fear. When I say that, I mean that whenever I fear a thing, I get on and defeat it. If it doesn't defy my physical ability, it doesn't kill me. Why do I have to fear it?

Life is all about what you make of it. If you surround your life with so much to be feared, you create much limitations in your life. Most of the fears we experience are due to what others may think of us. Often times we fear failure. Failure should rather propel us to do our best. There are always two things: it's either you win or you fail. The only way you will attempt to win is by trying or doing. You have already failed if you don't try. So, not doing is even worse than trying and failing. Now, when you try, you sure will discover your strength and weakness and possibly learn. If you don't try, you see yourself go down the hills forever wondering if or not you'd win if you did and still you will never win.

I grew up a very shy, timid girl looking people in the eye was terrifying and most times I will end up not saying what I wanted to say when I wanted to say it. Then I would end up very angry with myself and the situation that I couldn't handle. But over the time I learnt to confront it. If I aired my opinion, then I will feel better and no one was going to die either. Gradually, I would look myself in the mirror and spoke to the person I see. Now I can stand in the midst of hundreds and just say my views and then I knew I could win.

In my simple yet ambitious curiosity, I rather try than live a life of misery wondering how I could have performed. So, for me, to fear is only a medium to keep your life in a cage. Do it now when you can.

My three pieces of advice for startups:

Being an entrepreneur requires three major things.

1. **Passion** – this is the only thing that will keep you in business as every other thing including money will fail you.

2. **Be patient and aggressive at the same time.** You need patience for all the many times things are going to go wrong. You need to be aggressive enough to stand and pursue what is necessary for your growth.

3. **You must be self-motivated and resilient.** – A lot of things are going to go wrong. You will be broke, while friends and family are going to leave you. Do you have enough motivation within to carry on without the people closest to you? When

you don't have so much to keep up with demands are you resilient enough to hang on the rope of hope?

Skills for a successful millennial entrepreneur:

1. A good manager of everything. – people, time, resources and self.
2. You must be quick at learning new skills depending on your area of business. For me, I had to learn a lot about design quickly. Editing and all sorts of things I learned to do myself.
3. You must be competent with the computer and internet. These days one cannot over emphasise the value of a computer, the internet and social media to any form of business.

Becoming a Successful Entrepreneur

There's no pattern to becoming successful. If you know yourself, know where you're coming from, know where you're going to and you're prepared to get there. You will get there. It might take longer than you anticipated, but you will eventually reach there.

Building a successful customer base

Customers are very clever people. If you love what you do, they will know. If you're faking it, they will know. I've grown with my customer base because we didn't have enough funds. We grew organically, where almost every single customer knew me by my first name (or nickname Fauntee). I've been very authentic. They know what they see is what they get . There wasn't any faking it. I tell them when we're struggling. That authenticity has drawn so many people to our brand. Very many strangers have come up to me to pledge their support to help us get to the next level and they in turn have become part of our business family. That has been our magic.

Managing Expectation, Challenges and Reality in Building Healthy Relationship.

People say expectation ruins a relationship. But I tell you, expectation helps you determine your place in somebody's life. Having expectation in a relationship is like setting a goal in your life or business. It is a driving force which motivates you and keeps the energy of the vision for either your relationship or your purpose.

Bruce Lee said, "I'm not in this world to live up to your expectation and you're not in this world to live up to mine."

However, I would say, although no one should expect that you live up to their expectation, but,you need to know that, the frequency at which your expectation of a person meets at equilibrium with their reality determines the compatibility of that relationship.

The problem in human relationships is not expectation and of course, you do not have to lower your expectation to accommodate anyone's mediocrity. The problem is the motive or our inner feeling or the mind-set you already have about the other which is revealed when your expectation and their reality collide producing a result which you then react to. It is then this reaction that exposes your prior motive regardless of what you say.

Expectation is an essential ingredient in any relationship. It shapes the flow and tide the relationship takes. I want you to see expectation as a salt or pepper to be put in a soup. The salt or pepper is the expectation, and the pot of soup (quantity) is the reality. When the salt or pepper has been put in the soup, their collision automatically produces a result which is either a tasty soup or an over salted soup. When the soup is tasty, everyone will enjoy it and are happy, praising the cook. But the real test is when the result of the collision goes the other way. That is when the love you express for your spouse is tested.

Your level of expectation builds from how highly or closely you hold a person to your life. We tend to have much higher expectation of people we bring closer to us as family, friends etc.

Unfortunately we are usually wrong in our judgement of these people because we do not understand first our place in their own lives. My brother once told me, "it's not enough to say you're in love with someone. You need to also be certain that they are in love with you too. Otherwise you will soon be suffering a heartbreak." It is usually these misjudgements that create situations of disappointment.

Ask yourself, will you be disappointed with a stranger you have nothing to do with?

We expect that:

- What is important to us should be important to people around us.
- Our timings to be in line with that of our friends.
- We expect that our values will match with those of our allies.
- We expect that people will respond to or act as we expect.

But it is never these expectations that matter, rather it is your lack of giving them the benefit of the doubt considering you're not privy to all the backstories and challenges facing them. With genuine love in your heart, you would seek to understand why your friend have fallen short of your expectation rather than react in anger.

What you expect from life, people, your work, career etc gives an overall definition of who you are. We build our expectations from our own point of view, our experiences, beliefs. However, regardless of why and what you hold as your level of expectation in a situation, you also have to have at the back of your mind that you are dealing with human beings who are different, who react differently, cope differently and see the world also from their own perspectives.

TUNE IN

Tips for managing your expectations in relation with reality.

1. It's good to hope for the best but also prepare for the worse. It is good to hope for a particular outcome, however you must leave room for eventualities. Do not force it and avoid being overrun by negativities and worrying.
2. Regardless of your expectation of people, be open to the reactions you may get from them.
3. Be your own cheerleader. Do not base your feelings, self-worth and confidence on how people react towards you.
4. Avoid people whose values and life perspective are in parallel line with yours. Beware of people who only value you from the prism of their own definition of success. Just know who you are and never let anyone place your value at par with things as worthless as materials and objects.
5. Be truthful in a relationship. Say exactly what you mean and mean it.
6. Learn to say No and have no need to explain yourself.

SECTION SIX – 14 STEPS TO SUCCESS.

TUNE IN

Introduction

We all have our own definition of success. It is our definition of success which ultimately guides us to a part or route that we take. Understanding success in your own definition is crucial in making the leap to achieving it.

For me, success is about happiness and staying you in all things. It is about achieving your purpose and objective. It is inspiring someone, helping someone actualise his or her dream. It is doing that thing you believe will add a positive change to the world. Making this distinction helps you to focus.

In getting to whatever definition you have given to what success means to you. There are certain steps that remain critical for you to follow in other to achieve success. Below, I will be treating each step with you on the route to success.

TUNE IN

Steps to success: #1

Understand yourself

Self-knowledge is the most basic, yet most important step, to achieving success. Understanding who you are, how you are, where you are coming from and where you are heading to is very important. When you know who you are, you can confidently make decisions based on what you are aware of rather than what you feel.

Self-knowledge helps you to be able to criticise yourself while staying strong. It helps you to truly stay aware of your strengths and weaknesses. It equips you to face almost every situation without breaking the bows. You understand perfectly your excitement, your pains, your reactions and you are able to not let other people's views positive or negative distract your purpose.

Self-knowledge helps you continue to strive. It helps you to be as unique as you are. It helps you to confront your fears. It helps you to know your limits and help you to push beyond them. It takes you through the times of unbelieving and helps you to truly define your ideals and work accordingly.

How Do you discover yourself?

Self-discovery and knowledge is a gradual process. For some it could happen in a twinkle. For others it could take years of experience. However, self-discovery and knowledge is ever evolving. Self-discovery starts with observing yourself critically, yet friendly. Continue to analyse your reactions to situations. Keep a mental checklist of what you have accomplished and what you have not.

Keep an open mind. Have your own will, while knowing you are responsible for your actions. Taking up responsibility is the best and most effective way to truly discover yourself. We shall discuss this in depth as a topic of its own.

Try new things every day or as the opportunity strikes. You discover new possibilities whenever you try doing something new.

Continue to read and read. Reading helps you to understand your temperament, helps you to efficiently analyse your self-observation. It helps you to develop your mental capabilities and sense of judgement. For me reading can never be over emphasised.

My question to you today is this: who are you? Can you confidently list your five strengths and five weaknesses? Are you able to face them, either to grow in strength or to find a way to work around your weaknesses?

TUNE IN

Steps to success #2

Self Love and Acceptance.

Now you understand who you are what you can do and how far you can go. Are you ready to accept yourself as you are?

We often misinterpret self-love to be selfishness. No, it is not. Self-love is about appreciating who you are how you are even with all your flaws. When you begin to love yourself, you are less bothered by what is said... or not said. You are less bothered by other people's opinion of you. Not everyone is going to love you. Not everyone is going to say all the good things about you. So many people are going to misinterpret you and have several opinions of you. What does that matter when you are contented with who and what you are?

You are happier with what you have when you love yourself. You are content. This is the point when your happiness soars. Your smiles gets broad, your joy multiplies and you can just fly. Your confidence extends and your self-esteem grows. You see the spark in your eyes and your life begins.

Self-love can never be matched with anything. Your life goes beyond what you wear or what you possess. You are at home in your own skin. Naturally doors and windows of success begin to open wide and wide and wide for you. You see yourself slip in and out of the corridors of achievement.

When you love yourself, you are most likely to love those around you. You are more likely to share, to give and to take. It is totally impossible to love another person if you don't love yourself. Like Maya Angelou would say, be careful when a naked person offers you a shirt." Because no one ever gives what he hasn't got.

When you love yourself, your life begins to unfold and you can discover more talent that you never knew you had. Self-love is so powerful that you just shine!

Are you ready to shine? Then begin to appreciate who you are and how you are. Begin to appreciate your story and weave it into who you are because it is not what we have been through. It is what we have learnt from them. It is not how messy the mistakes we have made. It is how quickly we are ready to face them and make a change. It is not how much we've lost. It is how much we are eager to keep going with happiness and love.

Today is your another opportunity to pick yourself up from where you are, dust and clean and up then brace up, look in the mirror and tell yourself. I LOVE ME!!! Then see your light shine it's all within.

@fauntee.

TUNE IN

Steps To Success #3

Define Your Purpose.

Good morning; here we are again on our journey to achieving success. Are you ready yet?

What do you want to achieve? What is your goal, your aim, or your objective? Whatever your goal and whatever you choose to call it, it remains the same. Your purpose. What do you want from life and what are you willing to give back to life? Striking the balance between this perfectly defines your purpose.

We often don't realise how much we don't understand what and why we do some of the things we do. We are remote controlled by what happens around us in so many ways — the trend, our friends, and so many other things. We fail to truly grasp our personal purpose in life. So, my take this morning is to give it a real thought, to honestly let myself understand why I do what I do and what truly I want out of life. What is success to me? I hope you too will give it a go.

What you are up to today has it got any bearing towards your purpose?

What do you truly want from life and what are you willing to give back?

TUNE IN

Steps To Success #4

Start From Where You Are.

We often wait for the perfect time to go for our dreams. But unfortunately, there's never a perfect time. The perfect time is that moment you say, **'yes I can'** just like President Obama did. I admire his courage so much. We all have to learn from that. His critics went saying that he has never held any office of power. He does not have the qualification, he is not experienced and all that. But four years later, he sealed the corridor of power for the second time with the people's total approval. And indeed, he has remained one of America's unforgettable presidents.

Look at the point. When you are already down, are you going to fall again? What have you got to lose going after your dream? If you don't, then you are losing. If you did, there's chance that you will win. For me, I like to go with the direction that gives me another chance over what I already have. That is, if this direction gives me just life and death, and the other gives me life, death and better life. Then I will take the one that has offered me a chance to be better.

We all are talented and have something unique to give. Why not start from your strength? Then you will grow and definitely doors of other things you need will begin to open one at a time.

Take a chance today go for what you want with the much you have received. Let your light shine!!!

TUNE IN

Steps To Success #5

Give Your Best.

One thing is to do something, while another thing is doing a great thing. The difference between the good, the better and the best is always the little extra. Are you ready to go a little extra to achieve your goal? Remember that on our step four, the question was what are you willing to give? So, this extra is going even beyond that you are willing to give to give even more.

For instance, if you need to start a business in whatever industry, you need money but it is not forthcoming. But looking around you, you have all sorts of gadgets that you enjoy using. You may have to forgo them to be able to fund your business that you truly believe in. That's one right there. It goes to getting married and or going into relationship(s). Are you ready to play the fool? Are you ready to give only but your best? Are you ready to do everything in your power to make it a success?

When you are the best at what you do, people will travel from far and wide looking for you. Some of the greatest people known in the world are those who gave more, more and much more. Those who gave more than was expected. Those who wanted to give people better than themselves. You become great by giving the best of you.

When I finished at school of midwifery and arrived in Lagos, within one week, I started working in a small clinic in Mende

Maryland. When I joined the hospital, they were doing well but not great. As soon as I came, I observed certain things I thought were causing them not to be greater than they could potentially be. I made suggestions, and I worked very hard. I gave my all, and went beyond. Sometimes, I worked overtime to help other nurses. At the time, I was the most junior and newest nurse. But soon, I became the most relevant.

After about 6 months, I tendered my resignation as I got a job offer to join Havana Hospital which was a bigger and more specialist hospital. My Medical Director, Dr Ezeigwe, could not believe his eyes. he refused my resignation. One day he showed up in my house, he met with myself and my brother. Before my brother, Dr Ezeigwe begged me to not go, he offered to increase my salary. But I told him I wasn't leaving because of money but because Havana was a dream place if I had to practise nursing. He offered me to work part-time with them. But again I refused as I needed to focus on my new place and make sure I give them my best while I worked there.

While working as a nurse, as much as the profession wasn't my passion, I gave it my all at al times. It didn't matter how much I was paid. There was never a day I went to work late. I would arrive early, be on my feet and make sure my patients got the best I could give. At the end of each day, I always had a sense of fulfilment. It didn't matter that I didn't want to be a nurse, what mattered was who I was and what was in me to give to others. This attitude was a great help for me in learning so much in an environment that I never wanted.

The truth is, whatever you give to others finds its way back to you. Therefore, why not give the best of yourself so that something even greater than your best will find you?

Working in Havana Hospital under Dr Okeke taught me so much about running a business, how to separate fun from business. How to set your company values, policies, managing people and customer's expectations.

It was working as a nurse that gave me a window into having a meaningful professional interaction with people and by giving my best, I learnt a lot from them. When my application to go back to school was not approved by management, it was the best I gave that made my matron to give me an opportunity that was never available to other junior nurses.

My Matron's ability to understand my pain at the time and signing for my annual leave in December brought the opportunity for me to meet the guy who would today be my husband.

If one good turn deserves another, then one best turn must deserve much more and of course it does all the time.

Life itself is tough and so is everything in it. You must be willing to get tougher to achieve your success. It's all in your hands to give it your very best.

TUNE IN

Steps to Success #6

Surround Yourself With Like minds

Birds of a feather always flock together. When you have set your mind on a goal, however strong you may be, there are times when your gusto fails and all lights seem blink. These are times when you realise how necessary it is to stick with people who truly understand and appreciate your vision. These are people who will encourage you and give you the strength you require. They ooze the positive energy that you need at this point in time.

Honestly, you don't even need at all anyone who would not be there for you to encourage you because each little light quenched makes the road even darker and more slippery.

To succeed, you need not just people but the right people. Without meaningful relationships, you can't become anything of worth. Align your choice network of people with your vision and life purpose. Be in the midst of people who will push you to go beyond your limit and who are willing to catch you when you fall.

One of the first things that happened as soon as we began on the journey of building our business was people moving out of our lives. Many of our friends began to leave and avoid us. At first it was very painful as we became alone. We tried so hard to pull them along but the more we tried to take them along, the more they pulled away. Focusing on them became a baggage for us until we began to build new network of friends and associates who had the same mindset.

Sometimes we want to hang on to old friends, childhood friends and classmates. Unfortunately, as we grow, we discover our life's direction and some people are no longer going to fit in with our purpose and will have to drop off. Just as a tree sheds its leaves from season to season in other to stay productive, so is our lives. We must shed at a very point in time to stay focused. It will always be painful and disappointing but it's better to have a handful of healthy relationships that work than to have a million people around who would become baggages we carry.

When they say 'your network is your net-worth', don't take it as a cliche because it is not. Just like this book today wouldn't have been a reality if it wasn't for my connection with Vee Roberts. One day, I was sharing my thoughts on facebook as I usually do and she dropped a comment that will forever change the course of my life. Vee said, "Fauntee, why don't you turn these valuable contents into a book?" As soon as I read that, I got the jump and off the bed I went. I began to channel my words towards releasing this book. Within few days, I had gathered most of my works and Tune In was born.

It is important we take seriously who and what we allow into our space. our mind, our body, our thoughts and our being needs so much positivity to stay channeled towards actualising our life purpose. Words are powerful. Each word that comes out of the mouth of people around you will either make or break you. Therefore you must protect your space.

TUNE IN

Steps to success #7

Never Make Any Mistake Twice.

One thing I like about this life is; no matter how careful you are, no matter how much you know, and no matter how much experience you have acquired — everyone is bound to make mistakes. Don't worry when you make a mistake. It is not the end of the world. Mistakes sometimes are ways to sharpen our minds. When we make mistakes, we learn from it and what we learnt is what builds our experience savings.

Yes, make mistakes. I tell you, though, to never ever make the same mistake twice. The first will help you learn and you can come out of it. When you make the same mistake the second time, most likely it will be disastrous. Because you may never have the luxury of a way out.

The important thing always is to learn from every step that you take. Everything that happens to us is for a reason. It is a special situation that exposes us to the perfect learning process we require to succeed in whatever we do.

TUNE IN

Steps to success #8

Listen To Every Advice But Take Only Your Own.

You will mostly hear people say: "Don't listen to anyone, don't accept this advice, should you want to succeed." But for me, I tell you. Listen to what everyone has to say, but let your own advice be the final. Each word you hear has a part to play in your life, whether or not the one who says it is a friend or not. When people give you advice (solicited or unsolicited), listen first to every word they say. There may hidden wisdom inside their advice which you may never buy with money, got from experience or learn from school.

Every individual has gone through a process of living and in that process have gained experience in their own way. Knowing that you cannot go through every step to gain every experience so it's God's way of letting you hear it, know it without going through it. People's words have so much to say.

'Listen freely and open heartedly but take very sparingly any words of advice'

TUNE IN

Steps To Success #9

Always Have a Plan B

Success is one of the most trying things to achieve and so disappointments and mishaps are bound to be. There comes a time when it seems all roads have been blocked. Not giving up is the only option if you must get to your goal – Success.

Given the realities of life and unpredictability of our nature. It is wiser never to rely on any one plan. When you have just that plan, there's bound to be temptations on the way. I can't really explain it, but it is real. I, have found out that one plan deal is so difficult to come true.

If you rely on anyone, he is bound to disappoint you at the last minute. It may not be their fault, but still the same old temptation and life that we live in.

When you have a plan B, chances are that whatever causes the obstructions on your way may never be able to be on two ways at the same time. I hope you get my point. And when you have a second plan, you most likely will never be desperate over a thing.

Always have a backup to your files of every plan in all you do.

TUNE IN

Steps To Success #10.

Be Who You Are At All Times.

You are unbeatable when you are in your true element. The problem people often have is that we worry so much. We work so hard to create a persona that misrepresents us. Then, we attract the wrong people around us. We spend all our lifetime complaining about these people who: do not understand us, are not going where we are going, and have nothing of value to add to our dreams.

People often liken success to being arrogant, proud or snobbish. This is far from it. Be who you are at all times; have confidence in what you set your eyes on. People will at first despise you, but when they see you are moving on how you are, you will win them over. Originality is the point.

See, God is a great scientist and a perfect designer. His packaging of you can never be compared or equalled to any other. However you fake it, the real you will at some point overtake you. You would have created a personality problem for yourself. . All you may have gained from the fake persona will still go back to where it belonged in the first place.

The reality is that you are the only one that is you. Not your brother or friend can ever be you. Your uniqueness is what makes the world a very interesting and spiced up place to live in. Imagine a world without you? How incomplete?

Be you, do your thing your way!!!

TUNE IN

Steps to Success #11

Do Your Best And Leave The Rest

I call my husband 'the no panic magic man.' His words are always the same, "Baby, you have done all you can. Now leave the rest and let God fix it. But if you worry, that means there's something else you know you need to do and you haven't done it. Now use that energy to have it done."

In the absence of hard work and strategy we fret and worry. Unfortunately, worrying has never for once fixed a thing.

We worry about nothing. Things that do not exist. We distract ourselves from taking actions we need to get things done with our fears and worries.

Successful people are action-driven based on facts, while losers worry till their bones can no longer move.

TUNE IN

Steps to Success #12

Be Willing To Fail.

There's no shame in failure. We all fear failure and as such fail to attempt to achieve our dreams which in itself is the ultimate failure.

Embracing failure is the best teacher. Until you have failed in anything then you have not started. I always ask myself: what is the worst thing that would happen? If the answer is, it will not kill me or have me crippled, then I'm game on.

It is always from trying and failing that we learn to succeed. It might sound like a cliche, but I tell you that it is the biggest and best lesson you're ever going to learn.

I have failed in many things but have never stopped me from trying again and again. One of the many times that I have failed woefully, was when we first launched our magazine in 2012. I had done my best but my best was nowhere near good. I didn't have any idea of the industry. I didn't have the contacts, I never networked before starting and I didn't have any money. It was all passion and a vision with super hyped motivation that carried me.

On that fateful day after what I thought was enough social media promotion, only a handful of people turned up. It was a complete flop. All were a total disaster: the venue choice, promotion, guest list, organisation and management.

One year after, we did the anniversary of the magazine. It was a bit better than the launch but again it was a huge flop. 99.9% of those who attended that anniversary vowed never to have anything to do with us again. At the time, we were really scared of how we could move on without their support. But the drive and, the passion for our vision was stronger than any of such distractions. We believed strongly in what we wanted to achieve and do. And we kept walking.

Today, C. Hub Magazine has won several national and international awards. It was named most informative African Magazine in the US. It was shortlisted in the creative category for the great British entrepreneur award. And it is now read worldwide by over 2 million people every month.

TUNE IN

Steps to Success #13

Beware of Get Rich Quick Schemes

The grass always looks greener on the other end. Unfortunately, it never is except if there's someone diligently and consistently tending to and watering it.

Build on your experience rather than jumping from one end to another. It's easier and more exciting to do new things but it is smarter to stay the course.

I usually abhor network marketing, pyramid schemes, cryptocurrency ventures. You know those get rich quick hyped up schemes where people suddenly develop this manufactured confidence in telling lies. They tell you how many people have become millionaires doing what they are doing and you never quite see those people and they never quite become one of those millionaires.

Stick to what you know and become better at it. If you start out to be a publisher or a coach, become better at it. Become better at whatever you do. Do it over and over that it becomes part of you and it no longer feels like work.

Look at your business as building a legacy instead of a money making scheme. Get rich quick schemes will always come and go but great businesses will always thrive. Network marketing, pyramid schemes are designed to manipulate the weak, gives to the strong the little that the weak holds on to. People have and always will lose their hard earned penny to these schemes. Think of it, the energy, drive, time and enthusiasm you put to trying to convince people about schemes you don't understand. If you put 10% of that to developing your skills and building your business strategy, then you will soon be employing those who were luring you to the schemes.

TUNE IN

Steps To Success #14

Be Teachable: Learn From Your Juniors

Learning is about growth. There are only two people in the world; the learners and the non-learners. The learners are those commanding the affairs of the world. They are the successful ones.

Constantly learn from your juniors. The newcomers are always equipped with a wealth of new knowledge, latest ideas and trends in the industry. They are usually the undervalued, and people tend to look down on them yet, they have the most valuable asset for growth. A fruit that is ripe is only hanging onto the tree waiting to be harvested or or it rottens. Only a new one continues to grow and expand in size.

Admit when you're wrong, be humble. Be flexible and listen to others. Soon your ideas and skills will become obsolete and you will no longer be relevant. To make yourself relevant you must be able to learn, unlearn and relearn.

On Capitalism.

They lied to us.
They didn't tell us there was no way out of the rat race in a capitalist system.

For years and generations they've continued to lie to us. We — all of us — are still in the rat race. There's no getting out of it in a corrupt system such as capitalism. It is a system of survival of the fittest, a system of the jungle. You and I know that in the jungle, you are only as safe as your last meal. Even the dreaded 'Big Cats' are also hunted. How, then, can you be convinced that in a system where this is practiced that you can outsmart the race?

Growing up we were sold the myth of education is the lifeline to a successful happy life. We all went to school, worked so hard, came out best students in our area of choosing. You come out of school, and after school you need to gain experience. You again give your all, when finally you got the job. It may (or may not) be your dream job. Then the struggle begins.

Your life becomes all about the job. You're in constant fear of losing your job. You discover that your happy and successful life is as good as your last salary. It is never enough to solve your problems, regardless of what you earn. Your 'huge salary' is never proportionate to the ever rising inflation and currency devaluation. Inflation is at 200% increase and your salary if ever it gets, is on 1 to 10% increase. And when it does, you give thanks. You go for a celebratory shopping spree.

One month later, you find that your celebration was rather too early and exaggerated. You're back to adding and subtracting. You're having sleepless nights over what the forgone alternative would be in your list of all very important needs. House rent or car repair or hospital bill, children's school fees or is it food? Which needs to wait till next month?

They said that you aren't saving enough in your youth for your old age. Then, you look around. You see your hard working boss those days who preached and taught you to save for the rainy days and save for your pension. You wonder what happened to all of those savings that made him not enjoy a single day of his youth. You discover his savings for decades no longer worth peanut. Inflation and devaluation have made it impossible for his savings to give him the so preached security. There is no security in capitalism you see. It's all an illusion.

Then came the motivational speakers, Network marketers and all of that. They said, oh, if you invest you will continue to have yielding from your investment. They say you will have more time to yourself, you will be in control of your life, your future. They preach against 9 to 5 jobs. They say being an entrepreneur is better. Quit your job and have and run your own life. Build something for your kids, they said.

Again, you jumped on it. You have a dream; a vision of who you will become. Life will be easier. You will make more money and have time to do other things you love to do, have time to spend with your family. But they didn't tell you being an entrepreneur is a 24 hours job. When you start your own business, you will work till you drop. You will have to think, develop the strategy, learn the skills, be everything, from sales, to operation manager to customer services and marketing manager. You have to make the money to be able to pay yourself the salary you ran away from. You alone face the risk. They didn't mention all of that. They didn't.

They didn't tell you that you will lose friends and associates. You will be alone. You will walk a long, dry, lonely road for so long. . You will lose sleep thinking about what your next strategy would be. They didn't tell you how you would fear that after many sleepless nights and work, that at a snap of a finger your hard work could crumble and you are going to constantly hold it close like an egg. No! No one mentioned that.

They didn't tell you about the competition out there. The fight to satisfy and woo your customers to like your business over the others. They didn't warn you that you would need to learn to fake it, to lie through your teeth to keep being in business. They didn't tell you, you would have to also deceive others trying to persuade them to stay with you. They didn't tell you that capitalist success of making more money means you have to cheat and cut some corners. They never said that. They didn't tell you.

They didn't tell you that the supposed super rich had to cheat, sometimes kill generations to gain their dominance. Even when they do gain that dominance, they still live in constant fear of being run over. They didn't tell you.

They didn't tell you. They didn't tell you that you would work harder and longer, and take more risk than your 9 to 5 and that sometimes you're not sure where your next meal will come from. They didn't tell you there are government policies you must pay attention to and you are constantly going to be walking on an egg shell. They didn't tell you.

Now you know. Now you see, you see you're after all still running the same rat race like everyone else.

What's the point of this and what is the solution to all the lies?

The ultimate point and solution here is to arm you with the truth which will set you free. Set you free from the bombardment of illusions. The deceit of promise of a better life in money, in capitalism. There is no better life in living in fear of being hunted at any slightest mistake.

The real solution to a sustainable success lies within you and that is what no one is prepared to tell you because, it will not make them more money from you. You alone have the power to define your success and live within your terms of your defined success. The success you will ever enjoy is finding that which gives you joy at doing it regardless how much money it gives you. Doing what you love doing. If you love money, then do any legitimate work within the law to give you money and go ahead and spend it during your lifetime. If you love a conservative life, then go ahead and be happy with your chosen 9 to 5 job if you can find any or create small source of income generating business that will be enough to put food on your table. Knowing that no one is having it any better regardless of what they project. They also are secretly in debt just like you. The truth is everyone is owing someone somewhere.

If you love to design, write, speak, dance, run, whatever it is, do it for the joy of it. Do it because it gives you joy. Find every way to make yourself happy. At the end of the long day, we all are going to one day exit this world empty. I'm reminded of the wise saying by the wisest man that ever lived, 'Vanity upon vanity.'

What am I saying to you? Define your success, look for it and live as much happily as you can and never think yourself more successful than anyone or think anyone more successful than you. Stay prepared for your exit to the next life.

Stop working hard and stop working smart. Start working for the love of it, while working for your happiness and fulfillment

Mind Your Mind: My Mental Health Pledge

I pledge to myself:

To mind my mind at all times.

To not be strong but seek help before reaching my breaking point.

To take a break and move away from anything that threatens my mind, body and soul. It is perfectly right and for my own good to think myself first knowing if I'm not fixed I can't fix anyone else.

To speak up and speak out of my feelings so that people around me will understand what I'm going through.

To protect my space from any negative association of people, substance or activity.

I know that I will need my mind, as well as my body intact for me to achieve any success.

I will be woman who minds her mind.

TUNE IN

PHOTOGRAPHED BY PETER HOGAN

About the author.

Faustina Anyanwu (aka Fauntee), is an activist, author and serial entrepreneur. She famously said, "I vehemently refuse to accept that Black History should be based on slavery alone."

Faustina is the Co-founder and Chief Editor of C Hub Magazine and Pearlwoman magazine. She is the founder of the largest women of colour movement in the UK, Divas of Colour International

Women's forum. She is a renowned author, speaker and ardent advocate for women and fair representation of African story. She recently delivered a speech at the Tropics Magazine Summit in South Africa, where she spoke on, 'Exporting African culture, the best practice'.

Due to her eloquence, inspirational and unapologetic advocacy for women and African stories, Afrokanist magazine's editor compared her with personalities such as, Chimamanda Adichie, Maya Angelou, Oprah Winfrey and Michelle Obama, all of whom she acknowledges to be her icons and mentors.

Mrs Anyanwu was named most influential magazine editor and woman by Extra ordinary people's awards USA, was shortlisted in the Great British Entrepreneurs awards and was also named at number 8 on the Tropics Magazine's Africans Doers listing and at number 2 on the Afrokanist Magazine's African women in the UK. And recently she has been inducted into the African CEO's Hall Of Fame by African CEO Magazine.

www.ingramcontent.com/pod-product-compliance
Lightning Source LLC
Chambersburg PA
CBHW070425010526
44118CB00014B/1905